Group Counseling Leadership Skills for School Counselors

Group Counseling Leadership Skills for School Counselors

STRETCHING BEYOND INTERVENTIONS

THERESA COOGAN, Ph.D.

Campbell University

SAM STEEN, Ph.D.

George Mason University

 cognella®

SAN DIEGO

Bassim Hamadeh, CEO and Publisher
Amy Smith, Senior Project Editor
Rachel Kahn, Production Editor
Jess Estrella, Senior Graphic Designer
Trey Soto, Licensing Specialist
Natalie Piccotti, Director of Marketing
Kassie Graves, Senior Vice President of Editorial
Jamie Giganti, Director of Academic Publishing

Cover images copyright © 2021 iStockphoto LP/DrAfter123.

Printed in the United States of America.

3970 Sorrento Valley Blvd., Ste. 500, San Diego, CA 92121

BRIEF CONTENTS

DETAILED CONTENTS

CHAPTER 7   21st–Century Education: Technology, Expansion of Virtual School Settings, and Societal Hot Topics   102

CHAPTER 8   Activities and Resources   124

INTRODUCTION

Welcome! We're Glad You're Here!

Thank you for your interest in group work and group counseling! We are excited to engage with you as you read this book and invite continued practice, application, and dialogue around group work foundational knowledge and techniques, especially as they inform efficient and effective practice for counselors in a public PreK–12 school setting. We offer a perspective that may appear obvious after it is presented, but that, interestingly, is not commonly observed or researched in practice.

For those readers who are practicing or licensed/certified school counselors, we call upon the foundational knowledge you gleaned during your graduate school training in the area of group counseling. Most training programs in school counseling require one formal course in group counseling. Some training programs offer additional advanced group counseling courses or specialized group counseling courses specific to working in a school setting as elective options for their counselors-in-training. We know that culturally focused group work is a powerful venue school counselors can use to serve students, families, and communities. We also know that groups are running more often than most people realize on a daily basis in the PreK-12 school setting to meet prevention and intervention needs of students as well as the adults in the building and school community. We are excited to engage in this professional reflection and conversation with you by sharing a new framework, techniques, and information to support your success as a 21st-century school counselor who takes advantage of the far-reaching impact of groups beyond small group interventions.

You may worry that it has been forever since you were in graduate school or that your daily responsibilities as a school counselor do not have you engaged in group counseling with students. Or perhaps your graduate training did not include a required group counseling course, or the group course you did take was content driven and did not infuse skills practice or an experiential group requirement along with the content acquisition. Not to worry, we have you covered!

This book offers a practical, application-based approach intended for counselors from a variety of training backgrounds and current skill levels. The content and concepts in this book are also transferable to settings outside of a traditional American public school environment and are easily adaptable for a trained professional counselor.

Chapter 1 provides a summary of professional training and practice standards, which are constantly in flux. Chapter 2 provides a refresher on some key theoretical concepts and terms. Chapter 3 introduces a new framework, *TRATE My Group*, which has been designed to foster culturally engaged group work practices for task, psychoeducation, and counseling/growth groups. Chapters 4 through 7 will narrow the focus on a specific population commonly served in public PreK-12 school settings and illustrate how to apply this new framework. These chapters infuse current issues affecting the sociopolitical culture in the United States as well as public school environments, such as social justice advocacy, technological competence, and inclusive excellence with a myriad of stakeholders from various racial and cultural backgrounds that school counselors support on a daily basis. These chapters also present activities, prompts for counselor self-reflection, and scenarios to illustrate the application of the TRATE My Group framework. Finally, Chapter 8 wraps up with a repository of resources, articles, and professional development opportunities as well as activities that may be applied in multiple situations.

Background and the Big Picture

Inherent in groups and systems are unique complexities. Elements may be overt or appear hidden based on the perspective of each member in the group or system. In this way, we recognize that groups and complex systems, such as schools, are not linear. Small shifts in a process can generate different outcomes. Group leaders and counselors can use their advanced training as active listeners and knowledge of interpersonal and group dynamics to assist with guiding and leading groups through complex situations.

Schools are complex systems of groups that serve a variety of stakeholders at different levels. Each classroom comprises the teacher, students, and perhaps additional support staff; this is a "group" for that period(s) of the school day. The employees within the school building comprising the building principal, additional administrators, department chairs, teachers, and staff are a "group" of adults within that school building and school district. The employees at the central office within the school district, including the superintendent, school committee members, human resources, and staff, are a "group" for this district within the state. At every level, and from the lens of each stakeholder being served, both directly and indirectly, multiple groups can be identified on any given day in the U.S. PreK-12 public school setting.

Regardless of the building level or geographic location, a school counselor will collaboratively navigate, support, and often advocate for these groups on a daily basis as a part of their normal responsibilities in service to students, their families, and the larger school community. Acknowledging the complexity of relationships and situations that school counselors regularly work with, we suggest a framework and perspective to engage in productive, culturally responsive, and inclusive excellence. We invite you to consider implications for various roles (e.g., student, teacher, administrator, parent, etc.) from the perspective of group dynamics through an innovative framework called TRATE My Group that can be applied in any number of settings and with a variety of populations to support intentional planning, preparation, and facilitation of the work to be completed. In addition to offering practical applications to support the needs, partnerships, and work for the school counselor, we hope this book also serves to clarify the training, knowledge, skills, and capabilities of the professionally trained school counselor to more intentionally bring to action the power of groups in the school setting to foster growth, development, healing, and wins for all involved.

We hope that this book will serve as a professional development tool for school counselors as well as for the entire school community. For example, a building principal reading this book will likely not have completed a group work course during their educational administration training program. They will have likely completed leadership courses, however. This book may benefit building principals by drawing parallels through systems theory and group work theory that will bridge their existing knowledge about leadership into the daily and regular situations they oversee and are part of in the school building. It will also clarify for the building principal the multiple areas of training the school counselors in their building have, and in many instances are not utilizing.

The professional field of counseling is guided by a series of broad frameworks, models, and theories tailored to the specific specialty area of counseling. These not only guide and support practitioners, but they also serve to support the training of the next generation of counselors and the continual development of practitioners already in the field. For the field of school counseling, the five primary frameworks that guide our training and practice include the American School Counseling Association (ASCA) National Model for School Counseling Programs; the Council for Accreditation of Counseling and Related Education Programs (CACREP) Standards; the Association for Specialists in Group Work (ASGW) Guiding Principles for Group Work; and the ethical guidelines for practice of groups for both ASCA and the American Counseling Association (ACA). Some states also offer additional frameworks and models that further add to this robust collection of support for the practicing school counselor across the PreK-12 levels. Although not the focus of this book, we will reference these additional resources throughout the book as a cornerstone of providing and delivering ethical and professionally sound best practice as a counselor.

Who Is This Book Intended For?

Everyone! Groups invite inclusive collaboration and relationship building. As professional counselors, school counselors, and counselor educators, we wrote this book speaking directly to our colleagues in counseling roles for direct support and implication in their daily practice. That said, we intentionally present the content and examples in this book using inclusive language when possible and have worked diligently to make this book accessible to everyone who might be interested in using group work techniques and strategies to create group spaces that align with the vast diversity that exists in our schools and communities. We believe that even if an individual has not completed any level of formalized training in group work, they have life experiences as a member and possibly a leader of a group. These real-world examples might include, but are not limited to, being part of a sports team in high school or college, participating in a book club, volunteering with a church or religious service group, and even being a member of their own family. In this way, we will draw parallels with system theory as a way to understand group theory and dynamics to set the foundational knowledge of our new perspective on a group's applicability within schools.

For higher education faculty, this book will provide specific content related to the intended setting in which many or all of their students are seeking future employment upon completing their graduate program. This book will fill an existing gap in their course(s) such as Practicum, Internship, Group Counseling, Consultation and Collaboration, and Introduction to School Counseling as a supplemental reading that will provide practical application examples and context for class discussions and projects/assignments. We believe our ideas foster opportunities for the readers to engage in the material at a deeper level than is possible with a broad overview a course might accomplish while continuously empowering the individual's unique professional identity development to thrive.

A Focus on Group Process

The TRATE My Group framework will help school counselors and those who are in leadership roles to approach the daily group interactions they experience with a new perspective and increased intentionality on the larger process. *Process* focuses on the experiences occurring during and throughout interactions. As such, we can state that the process ultimately influences the outcomes. As a group leader, focusing on the process of your group, regardless of the content or purpose of the group, will have a direct influence on the outcomes. Conversely, focusing only on the *content* of a group, or what the task is exclusively, may or may not accomplish the task at hand, but the efficiency, culture, productivity, and future tasks to be accomplished will be unpredictable. For example, school principals may charge the school counseling office with addressing an increase in disciplinary actions that have been observed with the seventh-grade class in that academic year. Using a group work perspective applying the TRATE My Group framework, the school counselor can efficiently identify and proactively consider the effectiveness of various delivery systems (e.g., group counseling, classroom guidance and other psychoeducational groups, focus groups, etc.) that will maximize the resources available at that specific time and work toward the desired outcomes. We intentionally say "maximize the resources available at that specific time," acknowledging that the needs in a school building will ebb and flow, and that the same supports may not always be readily on hand or available to address every situation. Creative and adaptable flexibility is one of the essential skills of school counselors, while never compromising best practices or ethics. This framework embodies the realities of the work of the school counselor with an optimistic view that calls on all skill sets gleaned in a counselor's training. Therefore, process is a major component of all types of group work described hereafter.

We begin this book by acknowledging that practicing school counselors are already doing, completely or in part, much of what we suggest. Based on this assumption, we believe that the adaptation and integration of these suggestions will prove to be easier than considering a drastic change in practice. One of our goals is to support efficiency—"working smarter, not harder"—because the work of the school counselor is essential! We believe the suggestions for practical application suggested in this book will support your time and organizational management efforts as well as support your interpersonal relationships with both students and adults. Inherent in group work is collaboration and engagement with others. Through applying the suggestions we offer in this book, you will improve your communication, listening, critical thinking, and relationship skills. We invite you to reframe how you view the activities you engage in within your practice to more fully embrace the powerful group process. Many roles we engage in as school counselors are ambiguous. We hope to make using group work and group work techniques more normalized, inviting more practitioners to be culturally courageous group experts!

Professional Training and Practice Standards

Among school counselors, collaboration and working in groups or teams is often one of the most essential elements of professional practice, because the impact and effectiveness of a counseling team to serve an entire school building is powerful. It can be a natural part of the daily process for school counselors; however, we may not pause to recognize how these interactive group experiences are directly influencing and informing our work or consider how we can amplify the productive efforts by tapping into additional counseling knowledge and skills we have already gleaned through training. We understand and appreciate the need for efficient, effective, and intentional strategies and techniques grounded in ethical best practice. We acknowledge that there continues to be increasing trends in mental health needs across all levels and roles for children, adolescents, and their families. We understand that families are navigating even more challenges today than ever before, creating crises and struggles for the family system that can manifest for the children when they are in the school building. We also recognize that given the increased need for services to the students, families, and school community, our school counselors and other support personnel in the building are working even harder and for longer hours to try to keep up and meet students' needs.

Our framework taps into a skill set and knowledge base that all school counselors will have acquired as a standard part of their graduate-level training—group counseling and group work. Some may have had more training than others depending on the curriculum they completed in their graduate program, but it is assumed that all school counselors holding an active license for practice issued by their state to work in a public PreK-12 school have completed at least one course in group counseling or group work. While this continues to be a terrific modality for delivering effective services for intervention, we posit that with an open perspective, creativity, and flexibility (also essential traits and characteristics of a school counselor), we can transfer and adapt our foundational knowledge and skills in group counseling and group work to support school counselors in a wide variety of applications that are not solely intervention focused to serve students, families, and the school community. By repurposing and strengthening this existing knowledge and skill base, we are innovatively working smarter, not harder, to meet the needs of our schools and communities.

Our framework extends far beyond using group work skills to clinically diagnose mental health issues. We propose a perspective that conceptualizes how we define what groups look like and how they are used within the school setting as a strategic way to support effective and efficient work when a team of people is required to serve an identified group (commonly students, families, or the school community). One of the hallmarks of the professional school counselor is that they are trained in *both* prevention and intervention approaches, and our approach empowers its application to serve both approaches. All too often, frameworks and models in school settings and clinical settings focus solely on intervention. We strongly encourage this framework to be used to support intentional planning and preparation for any type of group, including department meetings for adults in the building or school committee meetings with community stakeholders (e.g., task groups); friendship skills among students or professional development training for adults in the building (e.g., psychoeducational groups); and self-esteem, anger management, or grief and bereavement groups for students (e.g., counseling/growth groups).

The TRATE My Group framework will invite the counselor or group leader to conduct a brief, yet meaningful analysis of the group they are preparing to lead. This analysis can be completed in as little as 5 minutes or invite collaborative discussions that can easily be adapted to short-term as well as complex group needs. The outcome of the analysis will provide the counselor or group leader with essential information that informs the **T**ype of group that is being planned or currently running, if the leader is transitioning into their role; the specific **R**ole(s) of the individuals who are a part of the experience directly and indirectly, accounting for all stages; the **A**udience(s) being served, often describing the specific membership (e.g., students, parents, administrators, teachers, etc.); the **T**imeline that can be anticipated for all elements of the process to occur; and, the **E**xpected outcomes from the group, acknowledging and supporting the evidenced-based practices that school counselors in the 21st century employ and inviting others to gather outcome data to support their practice with groups. Throughout each point of analysis, the counselor or group leader considers the evolving multicultural needs relative to their group and the other individuals directly and indirectly involved, as well as environmental factors. When we begin to invite an open perspective of "group" we can begin to see a myriad of applications, uses, and practices that have been happening for some time! Our goal with this book is to capitalize on the fact that groups are already in motion, and we know they work! We propose a framework to support this continued good work that will enable counselors (or whomever may be leading the group) to be as efficient and effective as possible.

Foundational Knowledge, Contextual Dimensions, and Practice

Throughout this book, several terms and concepts will be used that are common to the field of counseling and the practice of group counseling and group work. The following are essential terms and areas that will be discussed in this chapter:

1. Association for Specialists in Group Work (ASGW)
2. Group counseling and group work
3. Multicultural awareness (from the specific lens of a group worker)
4. American School Counseling Association (ASCA)
5. Council for Accreditation of Counseling and Related Education Programs (CACREP)
6. TRATE My Group framework

As stated on their website, the **Association for Specialists in Group Work (ASGW)**, is a division of the American Counseling Association (ASGW, n.d.). The ASGW states that they "exist so that members and other helping professionals are empowered with the knowledge, skills, and resources necessary to practice effective, socially just, and ethical group work in a diverse and global society." Benefits of ASGW membership include resources, training, and a subscription to its peer-reviewed journal, *Journal for Specialists in Group Work*. ASGW also authors resources to guide and assist the practicing counselor (regardless of specialization) who is engaged in ethical and best practices relevant for the group delivery mode. This organization is an essential resource and professional home for counselors as well as professionals in a variety of disciplines who engage in groups. Examples of other disciplines that may benefit from ASGW's resources include psychologists who practice in residential, hospital, or clinical settings; social workers, foster care staff, or child protective service personnel who facilitate trainings or interventions to meet the needs of the children and families they serve; or individuals in the legal field such as attorneys or justice advocates who may use group work to collaborate with teams of stakeholders based on a case or topic area.

The terms **group counseling** and **group work** are used throughout this book. While there may be times when the terms are used interchangeably, they do represent distinctly different applications using a group delivery approach. From the 1940s through the 1960s, significant contributions were made around the area of crisis intervention work. Findings have informed specializations in crisis interventions, grief and loss, and group counseling. Pioneers in the group delivery approach include Erich Lindemann and his colleagues who identified categories of crisis in the aftermath of a terrible fire at a nightclub in Boston, Massachusetts, that took nearly 500 lives in November 1942. Approximately 20 years later, Gerald Caplan expanded upon this work focused on crisis interventions and identified three classifications to describe types of groups that represent service of different levels of crisis: primary, secondary, tertiary. This classification system is still commonly referenced today in training and practice. *Primary groups* recognize a stressor or desire to change something that is present in one's life. Primary groups focus on the development of coping strategies and/or modifications to grow and develop in healthy adaptive ways that will seek to reduce stress or the perceived difficulty. Primary groups are often preventative and can be considered informative or educational, depending on the topic. Typically, these groups will have a clear purpose or topic identified before they begin and may be short (1 session) or long term (10+ sessions) in duration.

Secondary groups recognize an identified problem or area that is in need of change, growth, or development. The identified area may be mildly or moderately impacting the person's daily life.

It may be influenced by developmental delays that create a perceived disconnect with their peers, or it may be a coping strategy or intra- or interpersonal element that will benefit from intentional growth and development. Often, secondary groups will infuse elements of intervention and prevention; this balance will depend upon the topic. For example, a fairly common secondary group in a school setting is a self-esteem group, typically further differentiated by gender (e.g., a girls' group for self-esteem or a boys' group for self-esteem).

Finally, *tertiary groups* focus on severe challenges that are often more serious, many times including a pathology or a diagnosis from the *Diagnostic and Statistical Manual of Mental Disorders* (DSM-5; American Psychiatric Association [APA], 2013).

Commonly, the term *group counseling* will be used when referencing a tertiary group or an intervention- and treatment-focused group delivery format. Diving into the next layer of specificity, ASGW has recognized four types of groups or purposes for a group. These will be discussed in more detail in later chapters, but note here that they are *task, psychoeducational, counseling growth*, and *therapy/psychotherapy groups*. As we consider the typical context for the term *group counseling*, it is most often with reference to tertiary groups that would include the specific purposes of counseling growth, therapy, or psychotherapy. Often, when picturing these types of groups, we envision serving adults or older adolescents who may be in in-patient, residential, or outpatient settings. Because these groups usually involve members who have clinical mental health diagnoses and psychological challenges that significantly impact their daily living, the intention, purpose, and overall goals of the group are based on those clinical mental health needs.

Not all of these group types are commonly seen in a PreK-12 school setting. The structure, schedule, and typical resources available within a PreK-12 school is not suitable for delivery of tertiary counseling and psychotherapy groups or to address more severe clinical mental health issues. The broad goal for every student within the PreK-12 public school is to prioritize academic growth and development. Although career and social-emotional development are important and absolutely influence academic development, they are secondary to academics in the PreK-12 school setting. Thus, taking the amount of time needed to support and attend to clinical mental health issues is typically not feasible within the school environment. However, as more pressing social-emotional issues emerge in the aftermath to the 2020–2021 pandemic, the emphasis beyond academic development will increase.

Primary and secondary groups that are task based or that have a psychoeducational focus/purpose are more common in the PreK-12 school setting. These groups may be short or long term in duration; they may focus on fulfilling a prevention, intervention, or specific task need; they are flexible and inclusive, serving any audience from students through to and including adults; and they are flexible to open or closed structures based on the topic and goals identified. Simply put, these groups can accommodate the organized chaos that is a normative part of the culture and environment in a PreK-12 school setting and adapt to best serve and meet the needs of the stakeholders.

As we consider the use and context of the term *group work*, we can see how this term is used to encapsulate the myriad of techniques, strategies, and applications of working with and as a part of a team. As such, this term is not specific as to whether services are being delivered for a prevention or an intervention purpose. It focuses more on the act of tapping into a specific well of knowledge and skills to intentionally and effectively meet interpersonal goals with one or more people. We will usually use the term *group work* given the inclusivity of the term and diversity for application with both prevention and intervention applications.

What does it mean to have **multicultural awareness**? Diversity, in its broadest sense, acknowledges the uniqueness between individuals and groups. Notice that we do not offer a broad definition in terms of *similarities* and *differences*. Our choice of words here is intentional and helps to illustrate our point that we each bring different perspectives as a part of showing who we are and engaging in the various group levels around us on a daily basis. This is not as simple as offering a dichotomous scale when we are focused on meaningful engagement and processes with other individuals. As we consider diversity, we need to consider what we know, and accept that there is so much more we do not know. Through intentional and thoughtful interaction (e.g., through the group process), we have opportunities for interpersonal and intrapersonal growth and learning!

Individuals are part of multilevel systems that influence and shape their perspectives and interactions with others on a daily basis. This includes the micro-level of one's immediate family or those with one whom lives, up through the meso-level that includes relationships in one's neighborhood and community (e.g., teachers and peers at school, friends in the neighborhood, etc.), up to the exosystem level that includes the broader communities and organizations a person is a part of, and finally the all-encompassing macro-level that includes societal and cultural norms, values, and systems. This multilevel visual conceptualization is the basis of Urie Bronfenbrenner's bioecological theory that demonstrates the interactive nature and influences different system levels can have on an individual (Bronfenbrenner, 1986). In addition to the different levels of the system itself that can add complexity and diversity, one must also consider the complexity and diversity of each individual who is a part of the system and process. Although it may be among the first categories that come to mind, the term *multicultural* is not restricted to race or ethnicity. A variety of elements must be considered that comprise the identity of the unique individual in our intentional practice as a multiculturally aware counselor and group practitioner. This may include elements such as age, sexual orientation, gender, language or accents while speaking different languages, socioeconomic status, education, physical abilities or differences, religion or spirituality, and race and ethnicity. *Intersectionality*, a term coined by Kimberlé Crenshaw (1989), recognizes the interconnected nature of social categorizations, such as race, class, gender, and so forth, as they apply to a given individual or group that create overlapping and interdependent systems of privilege and oppression. Within the context of school settings, an understanding of intersectionality provides the multiculturally aware counselor a framework for how any of these elements influence and make up the identities of their students, families, and colleagues. Deeper understanding of intersectionality helps a culturally courageous counselor engage in their own ongoing self-reflection and awareness, as well supervision and continuing education, to learn more about themselves; to be mindful of how they change, grow, and develop as a person; and to recognize how that may inform their practice working with a myriad of people within a variety of groups.

THINK ABOUT IT ... LET'S REFLECT

- How many schools have you worked at over your career? Or, how many have you attended throughout your educational career?
- What does the term *intersectionality* mean to you? How does this term impact your understanding of group work within the schools you have worked?
- Reflect on how different each of these schools were with regard to demographics, leadership characteristics, and physical characteristics.
- To what extent did you reflect on your parents' and students' intersections of identity? What afforded you the opportunity to do so, or not?

It becomes clearer to see how environments, those you work with indirectly and directly, and the type of work/role you have can have an impact. The culture in the school impacts the individuals within it. Furthermore, the individuals and their intersections of identity also influence the school culture. This translates into how you and others interact and engage with each other, directly and indirectly.

Acknowledging the diversity described, and celebrating the developmental uniqueness that are present at all levels of the PreK-12 system, the integration of a framework centered in work with groups of people must be adaptable and flexible. The **TRATE My Group framework** is designed with this exact focus in mind and is intended to offer the professional field an adaptable tool supporting efficient and effective best practices, capitalizing on strengths and skills already employed by counselors. The framework is discussed in more detail in Chapter 3, but here's a quick snapshot of this mnemonic:

T – The **type** of group must be identified to most accurately identify goals for processes and roles.

R – The **role(s)** the leader(s) will play, and the roles that members hold or take on, must be identified. This includes the specific strategies, group skills, and leadership skills required for the group being planned. This is essential for guiding the implementation process.

A – The **audience** includes the members of the intended group as well as others who might not be present but who are invested in the group's success.

T – The **timeline** of the group includes the scheduling of group members, the projected schedule, and session details such as start and ending times.

E – The **expected outcomes** include those goals identified by the group at the onset, those the audience hope for, and those that might emerge as the group unfolds.

The counselor or group leader can quickly calculate and analyze a thoughtful understanding of the preparation, delivery, and evaluation of a group they are planning. Additionally, if a group is already in process, and the counselor notices that the group is stuck or less productive, this tool can be used to help the group leaders explicitly understand where they are in the process and identify solutions for meaningful change.

School counselors in the PreK-12 school setting utilize multiculturally sensitive awareness in their practice on a daily basis as they engage, interact, and serve a diverse group of students and families, as well as the teachers, administration, and other adults in the school building and community. Although strategies and techniques can be learned and developed with experience and efficacy in the role, the importance of this element of the work is infused in the formal graduate training process. Two key organizations—the **American School Counseling Association (ASCA)** and the **Council for Accreditation of Counseling and Related Education Programs (CACREP)**—help to inform and guide the foundation of school counselor graduate training programs to prepare multiculturally aware individuals and practitioners ready to serve and attend to a myriad of challenges on a daily basis, as well as celebrate and support the growth and successes that will occur.

Culturally Relevant and Ethically Sound Application of the TRATE My Group Framework

Nearly 30 years ago prominent scholars articulated that school counseling as a specialty area of counseling would continue to grow, develop, and evolve and would be impacted by various sociopolitical, educational, and ecological factors (Paisley & Borders, 1995). The rapid rate of change today makes it difficult to prepare school counselors for exactly what they will see in their respective school settings. Regardless of the times, school counselors are well prepared to engage in a myriad of activities within public schools. This is often a result of training programs that balance clinical skill training and knowledge with professional identity development. Two available resources that are well known throughout the country and world to help inform the training and development of the school counselor are the ASCA National Model for School Counseling and the current version of the CACREP standards, especially the school counseling specialization area standards. ASCA is an instrumental resource for in-service school counselors, and CACREP is an instrumental resource for preservice school counselor training, specifically graduate programs.

The ASCA is a national-level professional organization that serves professional counselors by providing for professional development, advocacy, and support for school counseling (ASCA, n.d.). It was formerly a division of the American Counseling Association (ACA), but separated in 2018, establishing itself as a separate organization independent of ACA, although the two organizations maintain a collaborative partnership. In addition to providing opportunities for continuing education and networking through a national-level professional organization, the ASCA published the ASCA National Model, which is a framework that articulates and guides best practices for school counselors' roles and responsibilities in the PreK-12 environment (in-service). The ASCA National Model launched in the early 2000s is on its fourth edition now.

Preservice Training and CACREP

CACREP is an independent accreditation body for related specialized program areas in higher education institutions recognized in the United States and holding approved regional accreditation in good standing (CACREP, n.d.). For school counseling master's degree programs, CACREP helps to inform the curriculum that comprises both content and clinical skill development minimums during the preparation and training phase in a graduate program and informs the learning environment where the training occurs (i.e., preservice). Note that CACREP accreditation is not required for school counselor graduate programs. In many states, completion of a CACREP-accredited graduate program is not a direct factor or requirement in the state-issued licensing process for school counseling. However, it does provide a recognized comprehensive training throughout the field at the national level, and will often have implications if the counselor intends to pursue another specialization later on (e.g., clinical mental health counseling) or a doctoral program, especially in the counselor education area.

Because families, communities, and schools are constantly transforming, school counselors will need to continue to be open to what lies ahead. School counselors are best prepared to do this when they have been exposed to comprehensive preparation and training. Although this does not require that CACREP or even practice and an understanding of the ASCA National Model be at the core of the preparation program, these two resources provide concrete examples that allow us to draw inferences about the preparation and training of the school counselor. Let's dive a little deeper into each of these areas and explore more about the influences and implications for preservice and in-service preparation as we consider the school counselor's role and how school counselors are prepared and equipped to understand, deliver, and evaluate effective groups and group counseling from a prevention and/or intervention perspective in the PreK-12 school setting.

Within the CACREP core domains for all specialties of counselor training, group counseling and group work is a requirement. At the master's level, counselors often complete one course in group counseling and have an expectation for group experience during the clinical experience requirement. During their practicum and internship, students accrue direct service hours. For many students, the majority of these hours are served in an individual counseling service setting, although some may engage in a group counseling experience. More often than not, the group experiences students will experience during practicum and internship are connected to the group supervision requirement typically facilitated by the university supervisor. According to the CACREP 2016 standards, "Practicum and Internship students participate in an average of 1.5 hours per week of group supervision on a regular schedule throughout the internship" (CACREP, 2016, Sections 3.I and 3.M). The challenge here is that the experience of being a group leader by the university supervisor may influence how this group supervision experience occurs. Typically, these sessions are held in a classroom at the university, which may unknowingly result in dynamics and a culture akin to a traditional class, rather than a group process and supervisory experience. This is one of the reasons why continuing education for site supervisors as well as university supervisors around group supervision is an asset and strongly encouraged! In these group supervision sessions, students should experience group membership as well as be able to process cases.

In some ways, the requirement for group supervision during the clinical experience can be a "part two" that builds on the knowledge, skills, and training experiences gleaned from when the counselor trainee completed the required group counseling class earlier in their program. The counselor trainee's self-awareness and engagement with others; ability to consider content and process, as well as give and receive feedback; and the overall goals of growth and development to be an effective counselor are enhanced from the hypothetical scenarios and class discussions from the earlier group counseling content class. CACREP provides guidelines on the overall learning outcomes for each student upon successfully completing their earlier group counseling content class. The summary of the 2016 CACREP standards related to group counseling presented in Table 1.1 shows how this scaffolded concept comes to life when we consider a counselor trainee beginning with the group counseling content course and then continue forward and consider learning and skill outcomes that might be expected in the group supervision class connected to the clinical practicum and internship experiences.

TABLE 1.1   CACREP Standards Related to Group Counseling

Upon completion of the group counseling course, students will have met the following professional standards through understanding knowledge/skills, including:
2.F.6.a. Theoretical foundations of group counseling and group work
2.F.6.b. Dynamics associated with group process and development
2.F.6.c. Therapeutic factors and how they contribute to group effectiveness
2.F.6.d. Characteristics and functions of effective group leaders
2.F.6.e. Approaches to group formation, including recruiting, screening, and selecting members
2.F.6.f. Types of groups and other considerations that affect conducting groups in varied settings
2.F.6.g. Ethical and culturally relevant strategies for designing and facilitating groups
2.F.6.h. Direct experiences in which students participate as group members in a small group activity, approved by the program, for a minimum of 10 clock hours over the course of one academic term

Source: CACREP. (2016). 2016 CACREP standards. https://www.cacrep.org/for-programs/2016-cacrep-standards/

As shown in Table 1.1, CACREP emphasizes a number of group counseling and group work objectives for counselors in training to understand and be able to do before completing their training program. These objectives are universal to support counselors-in-training preparing for any number of counseling specializations, including clinical mental health counseling, school counseling, career counseling, and rehabilitation counseling. Students who elect to attend a CACREP-accredited school counseling master's degree program will have acquired subject matter knowledge around group work as part of their preservice, and through their clinical supervised practicum and internship experiences they will have had brief opportunities to observe and practice these skills. We can assume that an introduction to group theory, group dynamics, therapeutic factors relevant for groups, ethical and culturally relevant leadership in groups, planning and selection of groups, and experiential opportunities have all been successfully completed, practiced, and learned. For those students who do not attend a CACREP-accredited counseling program, worry not! These learning objectives and the CACREP standards are publicly accessible on the organization's website. As a practitioner, setting your own learning goals for continued growth and development and engaging in continuing education that intentionally seeks to further develop areas that may benefit from additional focus is all within your reach!

In-Service Preparation and Support With ASCA

The ASCA supports school counselors' efforts to help students focus on academic, career, and social-emotional development so they achieve success in school and are prepared to lead fulfilling lives as responsible members of society. ASCA provides professional development, publications and other resources, research, and advocacy to school counselors around the globe. More specifically, the ASCA provides clarity on the roles that school counselors can take regarding the development, implementation, and evaluation of a comprehensive school counseling program. These resources can be helpful for training and preparation to enter the field as well as be resources to support practitioners once they are in their roles within the school settings. One of the ways they have helped school counselors to engage in evidenced-based practices is through the national model they created, the ASCA National Model, which is now in its fourth edition. The diamond-shaped diagram that illustrates the tenets of the ASCA National Model is included in Appendix A.

The ASCA National Model encourages school counselors to utilize the various delivery modes they are trained in to meet each student's needs (or other stakeholder they are serving) in the PreK-12 school setting. School counselors are able to provide preventative services as well as respond to interventions and crisis situations, when needed. Furthermore, they are able to respond to student needs through individual counseling sessions and group work.

Based on the structure and school environment, it is not uncommon for school counselors to find themselves implementing task groups (e.g., homework club) and psychoeducational intervention groups (e.g., lunch bunch or "banana splits" for children of divorce) (see Chapters 4, 5, and 6 for more on these types of groups in action). School counselors are able to use creativity to adapt the groups following best practices in group work to meet the needs of the students, presuming they have the support of their building administration to focus time on group work services. The intervention perspective is supported by ASCA within the ASCA Ethical Standards (ASCA, 2016). Section A.7 of this document is very detailed and provides solid information that addresses how groups are typically used within school settings, almost exclusively as interventions:

School counselors:

a. Facilitate short-term groups to address students' academic, career and/or social/emotional issues.

b. Inform parent/guardian(s) of student participation in a small group.

c. Screen students for group membership.

d. Use data to measure member needs to establish well-defined expectations of group members.

e. Communicate the aspiration of confidentiality as a group norm, while recognizing and working from the protective posture that confidentiality for minors in schools cannot be guaranteed.

f. Select topics for groups with the clear understanding that some topics are not suitable for groups in schools and accordingly take precautions to protect members from harm as a result of interactions with the group.

g. Facilitate groups from the framework of evidence-based or research-based practices.

h. Practice within their competence level and develop professional competence through training and supervision.

i. Measure the outcomes of group participation (participation, Mindsets & Behaviors and outcome data).

j. Provide necessary follow up with group members.

Elements informed by either the CACREP or ASCA can support preparation and training for future counselors. However, both leave significant untapped areas of development to expand content knowledge as well as skills regarding the group counseling domain. Additionally, where both elements do directly inform the acquisition of this area, it is from an intervention perspective. Expanding the knowledge base, skills development and application, and the perspectives to include prevention work as well as intervention work around the domain of groups are all areas to be enhanced and developed for the practicing school counselor. Our TRATE My Group framework is a creative and free solution to assist with these collective goals and is adaptable to any level within the PreK-12 setting.

We acknowledge the fluid and interchangeable use of the word *group* and we recognize this ambiguity even within training. For example, the group supervision requirements during the clinical practicum and internship experiences use the term *group*, but the way in which that experience is carried out may look drastically different between and among training programs, as well as between and among university supervisors. Some may run the "group" like a classroom, as if they are teaching a content class. Others might run the "group" in an unstructured manner that has no clear planning, focus, or process other than that the members and leader are at a designated location for a specified amount of time to talk about whatever concerns someone might bring that day. Given the ambiguity in training, it is not surprising that this ambiguity and fluidity with regard to the concept of "groups" often carries over into practice. Counselors who might enter a classroom to deliver what the ASCA National Model refers to as a "large group school counseling curriculum" can best position themselves for efficiency and effectiveness if they can train or retrain their brain to shift into the mindset of the class being a group (ASCA, 2019). This mental mindset can significantly impact the culture of this group before the lesson even begins.

The power of perspective before work begins, especially in a counseling process, is incredibly powerful. We often consider this from the lens of a client with examples easily identified when we look at resistance or blocks to the process, regardless of whether they are thoughts, feelings, or behaviors. As a counselor, we can adapt and shift our perspective anytime we are about to enter a situation or environment where we will be an active member or leader of what is truly a group dynamic and process. When we have our "counselor lens" on from the very beginning; we observe, consider, hear, react, interpret, and reflect on all of the verbal and nonverbal information that floods every individual in a different way than when we do not intentionally engage this perspective and skill. Let's take a closer look at an example application of the TRATE My Group framework that will show its flexibility and ability to provide helpful information to guide professional best practices even when only limited information is available.

Example Application of TRATE My Group

School Counselor Davis is preparing to push into Mrs. Ngyun's class to meet with the seventh graders she is teaching and deliver a school counseling core curriculum the school counseling department developed as the first step in a program to support transitioning to high school for the students. The program begins in seventh grade and carries through to the end of their eighth-grade year. Davis not only relies on the collaboration and support of their fellow counselors and support personnel in the school, but they will also rely heavily on the support of the administrators in the building, the teachers (Mrs. Ngyun specifically in this scenario), the department chair responsible for the content area that Mrs. Ngyun and the other identified classes are a part of, the parents of these seventh-grade students, and the students themselves. Whoa! That is a big group and a complex system of roles and members being served, directly and indirectly, just from one seemingly simple "push-in large-group school counseling core curriculum" plan.

It is not uncommon for roles or members served to be attended to only when they might be at the forefront. This, however, promotes a reactive process that can often come with additional stressors to manage or navigate, rather than the experience being a proactive process for all involved. In this scenario, Davis will apply the TRATE My Group framework to proactively and intentionally account for the type of group they will be leading, the various roles and audiences being served at all stages of the process, the timelines needed to complete each stage, and the overall expected outcomes so that Davis and the school counseling department can continue their evidenced-based practice efforts.

There are three resources that Davis may consider referencing as they consider setting themselves up for success in preparation for leading the large-group core curriculum in Mrs. Ngyun's class. Regardless of whether Davis completed a CACREP-accredited program or a program that directly infused the ASCA National Model as a resource during training, Davis can reference both resources to guide their planning and preparation now. Davis may reference CACREP more specifically to recall knowledge and skills for group counseling in a general and intervention-focused perspective, even if the unique contextual considerations are not directly aligned to the school setting. Additionally, Davis may reference the ASCA National Model for School Counseling programs to guide interventions specifically in this PreK-12 environment as they implement the ideal role and responsibility of the professional 21st-century school counselor. Finally, Davis may consider referencing the ASGW Professional Standards for the Training of Group Workers. The training and preparation of master's-level clinicians (regardless of specialization) has been described in detail in this document, which aims to provide guidance to counselor training programs regarding curriculum for counselor education programs training master's-level clinicians. The ASGW suggests that mastery of basic knowledge and skill in group work provides a foundation that specialty training can extend but does not qualify one to independently practice any group work specialty. To encourage program creativity in development of specialization training, the specialization guidelines do not prescribe minimum trainee competencies. Rather, the guidelines establish a framework within which programs can develop unique training experiences utilizing scientific foundations and best practices to achieve their training objectives. However, additional training beyond that acquired in a specific graduate program may be necessary for optimal diversity-competent, group work practice with a given population in a given setting. This principle can be applied to endless aspects of a school counselor's role.

Beyond these resources, Davis can explore the professional literature for peer-reviewed research. Although it is clear that groups in school settings are promoted as being effective at addressing a variety of issues for youngsters (ASCA, 2019), research-based evidence of their efficacy is scarce (Griffith et al., 2020). We have come to accept that school counseling programs should be developed according to the assessed needs at the school (Johnson & Johnson, 2003). Further, school counselors should select interventions that are evidence based (Dimmitt et al., 2007) and that use valid and reliable assessment procedures to evaluate their effectiveness (Steen & Kaffenberger, 2007; Studer et al., 2006). As school counselors collect data, they also must interpret the data and use it for program improvement and to inform their practice (Rowell, 2006).

Although the ASCA (2019) position statement on group counseling suggests that groups in school settings promote academic achievement and personal growth, more research is warranted concerning achievement outcomes (Zyromski et al., 2019). The literature base is still limited, and it is very difficult to facilitate group counseling interventions and to conduct studies with rigorous research designs, (e.g., large sample size, controlled studies, high treatment fidelity) (Griffith et al., 2020). Research that examines school counselors' use of evidence-based practices in school counseling is limited, and this includes, but is not limited to, group counseling interventions (Mullen et al., 2019).

The literature base in which to support the claims in our book are not always readily available. That being said, our collective expertise affords us the passion to pursue the manner in which to present these ideas that we use often and ongoing in many aspects of our professional school counseling endeavors. The *Professional School Counseling Journal (PSC)* welcomes article submissions that focus on practice from the field in order to attend to this research gap. The editor for this journal is a former practicing school counselor and now is serving as a school counselor educator. The editor's professional background and expertise provided the impetus for intentionally providing a venue for school counseling practice research. Authors who are interested can either follow the submission guidelines for *PSC* under the category "practice from the field" or can seek out the editor and request a mentor to help with the writing process. The practice from the field is not solely focused on group counseling; however, group counseling is an area that is still in need of additional areas of growth.

After exploring and referencing existing resources and literature, Davis can deploy the TRATE My Group framework to help them take what might appear to be abstract or secondary elements and bring them to the forefront in a meaningful and concrete way. This effort not only supports proactive and inclusive practice, it also helps Davis to ensure that they are as efficient as possible, maximizing the time they have to work with their direct-service audience (in this case, the seventh-grade students in Mrs. Ngyun's class). We have limited information to proceed with, and still, the TRATE My Group framework can be helpful to Davis. Let's break it down:

T – Type of group. We know that Davis will be facilitating a large-group core curriculum. Typically, these are psychoeducational in nature, but this will be an area that Davis will want to be certain to affirm *before* pushing into the classroom. As we will discuss in Chapter 2, there are different types of groups, and they all serve very different purposes and directly impact expected outcomes as well as the roles of the group members.

R – Role(s) the leader(s) and members hold or take on. This includes the specific strategies, group skills, and leadership skills required for the group being planned. This is essential for guiding the implementation process. We know that Davis will be the group leader and that the students are the group members. One lingering clarification needed is whether the teacher for the class, Mrs. Ngyun, will be a coleader or not. This is an area Davis will want to clarify *before* pushing into the classroom. Will the teacher be a coleader as the counselor uses the classroom setting to disseminate important information to the students? Preplanning and support to clarify the role and expectations with Mrs. Ngyun in advance will be helpful before the curriculum begins.

A – Audience, including direct and indirect members. We know that the students are direct members, but we also know that indirect members may also influence the success of this group. Indirect members may include the building administration, the department chair supervising Mrs. Ngyun, and the parents of the students. What information do these indirect stakeholders need to receive before, during, and/or after the group in order to best support the efforts and expected outcomes?

T – Timeline of the group. We know that this lesson is one part of a multisession program centered on the students' transition to high school. Clarification about the overall program timeline, the logistics pertaining to this specific session, and strategies in place for students who happen to be absent from school the day the session is delivered are all helpful preplanning, proactive, and intentional efforts Davis will want to explore *before* pushing into Mrs. Ngyun's class.

E – Expected outcomes. As a part of a school counseling department that is engaged in evidence-based practices, it is likely that the director of school counseling has identified goals for each session as well as for the overall program. In order to help realize these goals and directly engage in the overall process of the program and as a member of the school counseling department in the school, it will be important for Davis to clearly understand what the expected outcomes and goals are of this session that they are leading. Helping to clarify meaning is a powerful part of any process to invite inclusive, purposeful, and proactive engagement into a system, culture, or process.

Pulling It All Together

This chapter provided the reader an opportunity to reflect on the past and to get excited about the future. We began building our dictionary of key terms, concepts, and common language that will be used throughout this book and help to invite a universal language in practice. We began discussing the preservice and in-service influences and resources as well as current trends in school counseling as we consider application of the TRATE My Group framework to support efficient and effective practice of group work from a prevention and intervention lens.

All ages can benefit from intentional group work. Group work has a unique power to identify and make connections. It can invite group members to find meaning in themselves, in situations, and in relationships that they may not have seen without the support and power of the group. Group processes can affect all ages and types of people. A well-trained and well-prepared group leader is critical to the success of the group. We want to help you be that group leader as you continue engaging in your purposeful work as a school counselor impacting students, families, and the colleagues you work with in your school. We desire to get you excited about this concept that we have not seen written about in any other counseling-related book. We provide an organizational framework and expansive definition of group work application in every aspect of a school counselor's work.

DISCUSSION QUESTIONS

1. What was the biggest surprise in your work as a counselor/professional that caught you off-guard because it was not discussed in your training and preparation program?

2. Are you currently a member of ASCA or ACA? If so, which one? What about being a member enhances your work the most? If you are not a member of either organization, what is preventing you from being a member, other than the membership fee?

3. When perusing the ASGW website (https://asgw.org), what stands out as new information?

4. What are some specific barriers that might interfere with you infusing group work more intentionally in your school?

5. Apart from your school administration, who would you need to communicate with concerning your desire to infuse group work more fully into your comprehensive school counseling program?

6. Take a moment to think about someone who could serve as a mentor to you in your endeavors with regard to effective group work. Who comes to mind, and when do you plan to reach out?

REFERENCES

American Psychiatric Association. (2013). *Diagnostic and statistical manual of mental disorders* (5th ed.).

American School Counselors Association. (2016). *ASCA Ethical Standards for School Counselors.* https://www.schoolcounselor.org/getmedia/f041cbd0-7004-47a5-ba01-3a5d657c6743/Ethical-Standards.pdf

American School Counselors Association. (2019). *The ASCA National Model: A framework for school counseling programs* (4th ed.).

Association for Specialists in Group Work. (n.d.). *About.* https://asgw.org/about/

Bronfenbrenner, U. (1986). Ecology of the family as a context for human development. *Developmental Psychology, 22*(6), 723–742.

Council for Accreditation of Counseling and Related Educational Programs. (n.d.). *About CACREP.* https://www.cacrep.org

Council for Accreditation of Counseling and Related Educational Programs. (2015). *2016 CACREP standards.*

Dimmitt, C., Carey, J. C., & Hatch, T. (2007). *Evidence-based school counseling: Making a difference with data-driven practices.* SAGE Publishing.

Dubina, K. (2020, July). *How women and aging affect trends in labor force growth.* U.S. Bureau of Labor Statistics. https://www.bls.gov/spotlight/2020/how-women-and-aging-affect-trends-in-labor-force-growth/home.htm

Gladding, S. T. (2019). *Groups: A counseling specialty* (8th ed.). Pearson.

Griffith, C., Mariani, M., McMahon, H. G., Zyromski, B., & Greenspan, S. B. (2020). School counseling intervention research: A 10-year content analysis of ASCA- and ACA-affiliated journals. *Professional School Counseling, 23*(1), 1–12. https://doi.org/10.1177/2156759X19878700

Mullen, P. R., Stevens, H., & Chae, N. (2019). School counselors' attitudes toward evidence-based practices. *Professional School Counseling, 22*(1), 1–11. https://doi.org/10.1177/2156759X18823690

Paisley, P. O., & Borders, L. D. (1995). School counseling: An evolving specialty. *Journal of Counseling & Development, 74*(2), 150–153. https://doi.org/10.1002/j.1556-6676.1995.tb01840.x

Rowell, L. L. (2006). Action research and school counseling: Closing the gap between research and practice. *Professional School Counseling, 9*(5), 376–384.

Steen, S., & Kaffenberger, C.J. (2007). Integrating academic interventions into group counseling with elementary students. *Professional School Counseling, 10*(5), 516–519.

Studer, J. R., Oberman, A. H., & Womack, R. H. (2006). Producing evidence to show counseling effectiveness in the schools. *Professional School Counseling, 9*(4), 385–391. https://doi.org/10.1177/2156759X0500900405

Zyromski, B., Hudson, T. D., Baker, E., & Granello, D. H. (2019). Guidance counselors or school counselors: How the name of the profession influences perceptions of competence. *Professional School Counseling, 22*(1), 1–10.

Types of Groups and Essential Concepts

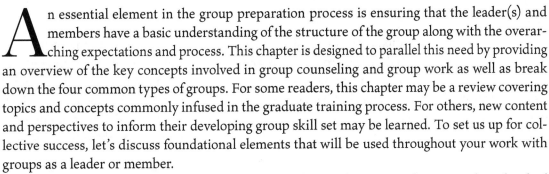

An essential element in the group preparation process is ensuring that the leader(s) and members have a basic understanding of the structure of the group along with the overarching expectations and process. This chapter is designed to parallel this need by providing an overview of the key concepts involved in group counseling and group work as well as break down the four common types of groups. For some readers, this chapter may be a review covering topics and concepts commonly infused in the graduate training process. For others, new content and perspectives to inform their developing group skill set may be learned. To set us up for collective success, let's discuss foundational elements that will be used throughout your work with groups as a leader or member.

A common misconception is that group counseling and group work are simply individual counseling skills, techniques, frameworks, etc. that are applied to more than one person simultaneously in a "group." Although we may see some similarities between individual counseling and group counseling when we consider skills, techniques, theories, and frameworks, their perspectives and paradigms differ. This chapter focuses specifically on group counseling and group work, defining key terms, noting therapeutic factors, and identifying roles to inform ethical best practices.

Foundational Knowledge, Contextual Dimensions, and Practice

This chapter builds on the foundation provided in Chapter 1 and addresses the following:

1. Essential logistics of group work
2. The four types of groups
3. Key terms, therapeutic factors, and goals in group counseling and group work
4. Communication, consultation, and collaboration within schools

Essential Group Work Logistics, Approaches, Terms, and Techniques

Independent of the school environment, several factors influence the logistical considerations and setup for group work and ultimately impact the group experience for both group leaders and members. The following factors tend to be considered universal factors for group counseling that are important for a group facilitator to consider before beginning to identify potential members or begin planning for their group. These factors include:

- Group size
- Format and type of group
- Membership
- Group duration and frequency

Each factor is explained in more detail below.

Group Size

The type of the group may dictate the optimal number of group members. Additionally, the size of the group may be informed by the group's goals and focus. For example, it is not uncommon for task groups that invites adults from outside of the school to be limited to four or five people. This may seem small at first glance, but depending upon the task at hand this may be a sufficient number for this group to be successful. On the other hand, a psychoeducational group of adolescents may find a group size of 8 to 10 students to be appropriate, particularly with a coleader (Gladding, 2019).

Group Format or Group Type

The format or type of group is often informed by the overall group goals or group purpose. The specific setting may also influence the type of group. For example, when considering a traditional public PreK-12 school setting, the group type of psychotherapy will not be a good fit based on factors, including, but not limited to, confidentiality requirements, time/scheduling constraints, and, often, a lack of resources or inconsistently available resources. As school counselors and school personnel in all roles are becoming more creative to find ways to meet needs within their buildings and districts with the resources they have, groups appear to be underutilized, which may be to a lack of personnel trained in group counseling and group work within the building or, more likely, due to the traditional perspective of group counseling in a therapeutic/psychotherapy format being a limiting factor.

As we consider the 21st-century school setting, culture, and environment, we can see how counselors and other personnel within the school building may already be creatively, intentionally, and organically using groups within the school settings—they just may not be labeling it as "group work." This label, however, can provide additional focus for a counselor in their direct work and/or through consultative efforts with others in the building who will likely not have completed any formal graduate-level training in groups or group counseling. For trained counselors, the label of "group work" can open up an entire tool box of information, techniques, and skills that they have available to support effective and efficient work.

To get started with identifying which type of group is the best fit, or to identify which type of group is already in motion, it may help to look at some of the other features of the group. The following are a few example questions that can be asked to determine the proper group format or group type:

- Is the group open to all or is it closed?
- Will members need to be recruited, or are there already enough (or more than enough) members to form the group? In other words, how many people can best be served through the use of a group format?
- Will this group be best supported by having two coleaders, if the resources support this option? Would coleaders enable a greater frequency of group sessions or aid in active group processes?
- Is the group's purpose to deliver information or to solve a problem? Or is the group's purpose to offer a space for support and reflection of feelings?
- Is the topic appropriate for a school setting? Are resources available to provide support and assistance to the leader and the members, as needed?

Identifying the purpose of the group helps to determine the specific type of group that might be best for the participants. Let's dive a bit deeper into these areas.

Group Membership

Group membership essentially entails determining who is being targeted or chosen for participation in the group. Determining the appropriate group membership could entail first deciding whether the group is voluntary or whether it is required/mandated. It may also involve determining whether the participants will identify themselves for participation or whether it will be necessary to recruit and reach out to the candidates. Developmental considerations may need to be considered regarding the members selected based on other factors to be addressed during group sessions. Developmental factors may also overlap with group duration and frequency. For example, the attention span and focus of an adult is commonly accepted as being longer than that of children younger than 15 years. In addition, children may reach their attention capacity after just a few minutes when groups are facilitated virtually in comparison to those conducted face to face.

Group Duration and Frequency

In most cases, group duration and frequency—that is, how often the group will meet, for how many sessions, and the duration of each meeting—are determined prior to the commencement of the group. Group duration and frequency may be dictated based on an emerging need (e.g., crisis response teams) or it may be a standing group (e.g., monthly administration team meetings) that occur on a predetermined day and time following a rotating schedule, such as the last Thursday of each month from 3:30 p.m. to 5:00 p.m.

All of these factors can influence the overall group dynamics and the ways in which the individuals who are a part of the group and external to the group interact. Group dynamics include the norms and patterns of acceptable and unacceptable behaviors that are identified and valued by the group. It may include the communication styles and modes used by group members among themselves, as well as how they communicate with individuals external to the group, which may be more necessary for task groups. It may include the ability and potential for cohesion to develop among group members or how the membership is perceived as part of the self-concept as well as external perceptions. Does being a part of this group contribute or influence the perceived status of the member? This may be more influential for children who are developmentally navigating stages where peers' perceptions and recognition are important than it would be for an adult. For example, a child interested in joining an after-school foreign language club may be reluctant to join if they perceive that their status of being a member of that group will be negatively perceived by their peers. Take a similar situation, but shift it to a collegiate environment. Based on a different normative stage of development (cognitive and emotional, most specifically), we presume that a college student will have a stronger sense of self and be less concerned with the perceptions of others if they choose to join a foreign language club. Motivation factors tend to become more intrinsic as development progresses from external factors more commonly observed among younger children. This is important for adults to bear in mind because they have already gone through this developmental transition themselves; however, the children have not yet made the journey. For them, peer perception often is an important and critical influence.

Group Terms

As in any discipline, group work and group counseling has developed its own vocabulary to guide this work. A key terms box is provided below that will be most relevant to group work and counseling in a school setting. Terms such as *group dynamics*, *group process*, and *therapeutic factors* often are used to inform a group leader or to consult with a colleague. In addition, four types of groups are typically identified: *task, psychoeducational, counseling,* and *therapy* (DeLucia-Waack, 2006). We will drill down a step further to identify key phases or stages of a group that illustrate where on the timeline a group may be in their work. These *group phases* are called by several names, but we will refer to them in their simplest nature: *beginning, middle,* and *ending stages.*

Group members' collective dynamics and active engagement will change/transition in every stage, and in any approach to group work, will be unique. Inherent in the group process is a level of unpredictability, given that it involves dealing with unique individuals. This said, group leaders, and professionals who are applying a group work approach to support effective and efficient best practices may be aided in their work by considering general commonalities. For example, regardless of the type of group approach used, most members in the *beginning* stage of a group will experience anxiety, stress, or uncertainty about what is to come and what their role may be in the group. To address this, as well as to maintain effective and efficient best practices, group leaders often will spend the first group meeting discussing with the group the group's purpose, the role each person has as a member of the group, how group members were selected or why they may be required to be a part of this group, and how long the group will be meeting and where. In addition, if there are predetermined objectives or goals for the group, these will often be presented and discussed. Group leaders often are able to invite interaction and input from each member to contribute in their own wording what the *group rules* and *group norms* will be.

As we consider the type of group approach used, we also need to consider the impact of the group leader and their leadership style. Different types of group approaches will be better served and illicit different dynamics based on the leadership style employed. We will talk more about group leadership style and practical applications to support efficient and effective practice using the TRATE My Group framework in later chapters of this book as well. First, let us define and briefly discuss the four types of group work commonly used.

The Four Common Types of Groups

Task Groups

Task groups are also referred to as *education groups* in certain settings. Some may even consider these to be committees or leadership teams. The essential tenets of a task group are as follows:

- The group has a particular goal or goals, which may be prescribed before membership is defined or created by the membership once assembled.
- Membership requirements are clear. It can be a *closed* group, whereby the members are identified and remain static until the task is accomplished, or it can be an *open* group, whereby initial members to start the group are identified but they may leave and be replaced or additional members may join, keeping the membership dynamic.
- The majority of the group's time is spent focused on the specific task at hand (this often occurs during the middle stage of other group approaches).
- The duration of the group can vary, and is often dependent on the completion of the required task.

Psychoeducational Groups

Oftentimes when people think of group work with children and adolescents in a PreK-12 school setting, they are likely thinking of a psychoeducational group (DeLucia-Waack, 2006). Psychoeducational groups are most often broad and far-reaching with regard to the audiences served and topics covered. Psychoeducational groups blend prevention and intervention work. They invite semi-structured formats to have a specific goal or task or theme in mind, yet maintain the freedom to flow with the needs of the group more than would commonly be seen in a task group. In this way, they are often easily facilitated by group leaders ranging in skill level and experience. This is, in part, because most psychoeducational groups provide continual opportunities for individual members, as well as the group as a unit, to learn, reflect, and make meaning from their experiences in the group. The experiences are explored and discussed as they are happening in real time during group sessions—what is often referred to as "focusing on the present" or the "here and now." The experiences may also be explored and discussed as members reflect and draw connections between past sessions or draw connections for something that is planned for the future. Psychoeducational groups can take the form of small group counseling sessions, classroom guidance lessons, or even after-school clubs. Psychoeducational groups can adapt to the members being served, can be any number of sessions in length, and can infuse several therapeutic factors based on the topic and the training/skill level of the group leader. Psychoeducational groups seen in PreK-12 schools often have topic themes such as friendship building and social skills, career exploration and planning, and academic success and study skills.

Counseling and Growth Groups

Counseling and growth groups may occur in the school setting or in clinical or residential counseling settings. Counseling groups absorb all of the traits and possibilities that task and psychoeducational groups offer and continue beyond them to offer an even deeper level of service. Counseling groups can be planned to serve students as well as adults. Depending on the training and resources available within a particular PreK-12 school (both at the building and district levels), the counseling groups offered will vary across building levels. Counseling groups offered at the high school level often address the cognitive, emotional, and behavioral development of the members served. Adolescents are more apt to engage in abstract thinking than elementary- or middle school–aged children based on normative stages of brain and cognitive development (Broderick & Blewitt, 2020). Counseling groups may focus on prevention or intervention, and will intentionally focus on creating opportunities for each member to engage in the group process, informing their learning, growth, and meaningful experience as an individual as well as in their role as a key member of that group. The titles of groups for elementary school students may be more creative than those serving high schoolers. For example, groups that are designed and facilitated by school counselors to support children at the elementary level whose parents are at any stage of divorce are commonly called *banana splits groups*. At the high school level, this topic is more likely to be addressed in individual sessions with the adolescent rather than as part of a group delivery mode. Topics commonly addressed by counseling groups targeted at adolescents include anger management; self-esteem; and changes that impact the family, such as divorce, parents/siblings who are incarcerated, substance abuse, and transitions.

Therapy Groups

Therapy groups are the most intensive of the four group types and will typically include membership from adolescents through adults. These groups often have key topics or themes and are focused on therapeutic goals for each individual member. These groups are more commonly offered in an outpatient setting or residential group home or hospital. Therapy groups are not as common in the PreK-12 school setting. Examples of topics that inform therapy groups include trauma, marriage/relationships, abuse (domestic, substance, self-harm), or stress/social anxiety. Although it is not to say that children and adolescents are immune from experiencing challenges and topics that may be aided by participation in a therapy group, the nature of the therapy group typically does not align with the schedule and environment of the PreK-12 school setting. Remembering that the students are in the school building to focus on academic development as their primary task, and recognizing that life outside of school does impact academic success (both in adaptive ways as well as adding barriers), asking a student to open that wound in the school building to do the work for a very brief amount of time is not supporting the group process or the student. Furthermore, many school support personnel, including school counselors, have not been trained at an advanced level in group work and group leadership to be prepared to plan and facilitate a therapy group in the school setting.

KEY TERMS AND MAKING SENSE OF THEM

Confidentiality: In the counseling and therapy field, confidentiality is the ethical principle of refraining from disclosing content discussed during the counseling process with anyone other than the client or a direct supervisor. The American Counseling Association code of ethics and the American School Counselors Association ethical best practices reference specific circumstances in which confidentiality can be breached to protect the safety of the client, another person the client may have contact with, or if there is a court-ordered subpoena. In school settings, everything discussed must be treated with the utmost confidentiality; however, it is acknowledged that it is difficult to maintain confidentiality when working with children, and adolescents especially. A suggested group rule leaders can deploy to seek buy-in from the members during prescreening and the initial session is, "What's *said* in group *stays* in group; what's *learned* in group, *leaves* group." This rule acknowledges reality, but does so in an adaptive manner and focuses on encouraging skill and growth development based on what each individual learns as a part of the group experience and process while simultaneously respecting the privacy of other members' contributions to the group.

Conflict in group counseling: Critical moments may occur between individual members and/or the group as a whole within the group process. Within this context, conflict is a normal and desired goal to bring into the here-and-now anxieties, unresolved interpersonal issues, or maladaptive behaviors that are affecting interpersonal relationships. Such conflict is not aggressive or violent, and it is likely to only occur when the group culture is one of cohesion, safety, and trust to engage in open dialogue that invites learning, growth, and change. It is the leader's responsibility to create a safe and productive environment for the group to work toward this normative element within the group process.

Critical incident: A critical incident is a peak experience for an individual member, a small subgroup of members, and/or the group as a whole that serves as a catalyst for growth, change, or new insights. This experience is informed by several factors, including, but not limited to, the group's type, format, topic/purpose, membership, communication and interpersonal dynamics or cohesion among the group members, and other group elements. This experience may be experienced and/or witnessed within one session or at a later phase in a group that has multiple sessions, again based on several factors, as described above. Groups may identify more than one critical incident.

Group content: This is the "what"; the topic that is being discussed, worked on, and explored during group work.

Group dynamics: The observed direct and indirect interactions and experiences of the group members and the group leader.

Group membership: The group membership is who is a part of the group. This includes each member of the group who participates in the group experience as well as the group leader(s). There may be one or two group leaders for any of the four types of groups described based on a number of variables (e.g., experience, training, resources, size of the group, etc.).

Group norms: What the group accepts as the parameters that will guide behavioral interactions and engagement in the group. Often determined by the group during the first session. Norms often address expectations for verbal and nonverbal participation and outcomes for being late or missing a session. Any number of norms may be identified, depending largely on the group topic and the group membership.

Group phases: A way of understanding the point in time of where the group experience is. Phases often are classified in a general sense of *beginning*, *middle*, and *end* based on the overall group objectives. Based on the type of group, group phases can be determined by the group dynamics such that as the dynamics and engagement increase, the phases progress. The group phase can also be determined by a task/action/goal of the group, whereby the phases progress as the group builds toward completion of a particular task/action/goal. No matter the duration of the group or the type of group, there is always movement through these foundational phases.

Group process: The "how" of the group; often informed by inter- and intrapersonal dynamics.

Group rules: Similar to group norms, rules often are determined by the group during the first session. Some rules may be nonnegotiable and established by the group leader to ensure the safety of each group member, such as "No physical or verbal harm such as hitting or swearing in the group." When such rules are preset, it is recommended to have them already written and prominently displayed even before the first member steps into the room so that it clearly shows that it is a static rule and was not created on the fly.

Informed assent: Similar to informed consent, which counselors use with adults, informed assent is used with minors or adults who are not legally able to make decisions on their own behalf. To obtain informed assent, the counselor seeks to affirm that the minor understands the expectations, benefits, and possible risks of engaging in the group.

Informed consent: The counselor is responsible to obtain informed consent from an adult who is of sound mind and able to make informed decisions about their life. The intention is to explain all expectations, rights, and anticipated benefits and risks and to ensure that there is no coercion or misunderstandings before the counseling process begins. This is often completed through a verbal conversation and a document that summarizes all of the elements discussed that is signed as the evidence of the client providing their informed consent to participate in counseling.

Outcome evaluation: An approach to assess and determine the effectiveness of the group by evaluating the results, such as whether change has occurred or how change can be measured. Outcome evaluations often are administered at the completion of the end phase of the group process and may or may not be informed by pretest measures. Outcome evaluation, which is sometimes referred to as *impact evaluation*, can be helpful to assess whether concrete goals and tasks have been achieved.

Process evaluation: one approach to assess and determine the effectiveness of the group's process. Process evaluation will look at a variety of perspectives while the group is in process exploring the evolution of the group and identifying contributing factors and events that appeared to impact the culture and overall experience in the group. As the name implies, this evaluation method focuses on the process of how the group is delivered.

Process observation: This may be a unique and distinct person and role (known as a *process observer*), or it could be an invitation for any member of the group (members and/or leaders) to offer. Depending on the structure of the group, process observations may be woven throughout a session as they happen, or they may be held until the end of the session as a part of wrapping up that specific day/session. When a distinct process observer is a part of a group, they will often sit outside of the group circle, similar to a fish bowl structure, to allow them to observe objectively and entirely. It also tends to be less distracting to the group members when this type of separation is engaged. The purpose of process observation is to examine and offer to the group what the experiences and dynamics are of the groups and its members. A universal goal when using process observations is to contribute to the overall effectiveness and efficiency of the group process. When there is not a distinct person serving as a process observer for the group whose sole responsibility is to continuously observe throughout the entire group, this responsibility is absorbed by the group leader(s). When there are coleaders, one leader often will take a more central role in process observation as a way of dividing responsibilities and focus. Beginning group leaders are encouraged to invite an experienced group leader to serve as a process observer as a way of enhancing their development as a group leader, as well as contributing to the direct group process.

Yalom's Therapeutic Factors (Yalom, 1995, 2005; Yalom & Leszcz, 2020)

Altruism: The positive feelings that a member may experience when they are helping others.

Catharsis: An emotional outpouring illustrative of one's experience; feeling a sense of relief or that a weighted burden has been released.

Corrective recapitulation of the primary family group: Reflection of a member's role within their family of origin that ends up playing out (consciously or unconsciously) in the group experience.

Development of socializing techniques: Openly listening and hearing suggestions or feedback in a nondefensive manner shared by group members about a life problem a person is struggling with or an area that may be identified as needing further exploration or change.

Existential factors: Reflection of life's meaning and one's role within their life.

Group cohesion: The rapport and relationship that is built to engage members in the group process.

Imitative behaviors: Intentionally choosing to adopt behaviors observed by another member or the leader of the group that are viewed as appropriate, healthy, and/or desired such that the group experience becomes a safe place to "practice."

Imparting information: Learning and gaining insight about the immediate challenge/task/action that needs to be accomplished.

Instillation of hope: Positive feelings and unique inspirational thoughts that occur from observing others and vicariously learning from others during the group process as they improve, navigate, and problem-solve as they work on their own goals.

Interpersonal learning: Clarity and new realizations about how the member comes across to other individuals; learning or awareness about the impression usually made on others.

Universality: The experience in a group that occurs when a member no longer feels like they are all alone.

In addition to the highly regarded therapeutic factors identified by group work pioneer Dr. Irvin Yalom, an alternate perspective is offered by Corey, Corey, and Corey (2018), who proposed 13 therapeutic factors that inform group dynamics and processes: self-disclosure, feedback, confrontation, cohesion and universality, hope, willingness to risk and trust, caring and acceptance, power, catharsis, cognitive component, commitment to change, freedom to experiment, and humor. Although these therapeutic factors are mostly focused on the process and dynamics that inform group members' experience, development, and growth, they also have implications for group leaders. For example, self-disclosure may speak to a member's willingness to engage in sharing personal successes and challenges as a part of the group experience. It may also speak to a group leader modeling appropriate self-disclosure for the entire group. When leaders do this, it must be strategic to support a specific purpose in the group, which distinguishes it from member self-disclosure. Similarly, feedback may inform both members and leaders, offering slightly different, yet still critical, distinguishing features of use.

We seek to build on this solid foundation established by reputable practitioners and researchers and offer our own maxims or factors that inform group dynamics and processes beyond intervention and clinical application. The following factors will inform the entire TRATE My Group framework presented in this book as another set of tools for practitioners in school settings and beyond:

- **Book your own reservation (with room for guests to join).** Even in group situations, our primary focus and responsibility needs to be on ourselves. We can take accountability, responsibility, and ownership for our actions and inactions. This does not ignore caretaking responsibilities; rather, the idea here is similar to the adage when traveling on an airplane: "Put your own oxygen mask on first before helping others." Airlines tell parents and adults caring for a child or someone in need of additional assistance to put their own oxygen masks on first. We can metaphorically take the same action when it comes to being a part of a group. If we each take the responsibility to "book our own reservation," we assume the responsibility and make the intentional decision to be an active part of the group no matter what one's role is. Through this action, we acknowledge openly that we plan to be actively present to the best of each of our unique abilities. We make no excuses or try to avoid the inevitable; that is, there may be situations, contexts, or circumstances that may be challenging or make it difficult for us to "show up," but by booking our own reservation, we commit to being a part of the process. If each person focuses on their own self to ensure that they are actively present for all aspects of the group process, then the group can focus sooner on the process and the content goals they have.

- **Validate, even if you can't relate.** For one individual to be able to truly validate another, they must be present and completely open in the communication and relationship with another person or group. It requires intentionality and vulnerability to truly be with another person or group of people in real time, undistracted by anything else, and truly focused on what another is saying or doing. In counselor training, we discuss the importance of differentiating between *sympathy* and *empathy*. The former takes all parties involved to a shared emotional state, commonly comprising negative, stressful, sad, or anxious feelings, whereas the latter refers to the deeper connection and comprehension of the subjective and personalized experience or world of another or others (Meier & Davis, 2019). A common metaphor used in training sets the stage: When your client is stuck in a hole, and you, as the counselor are standing on the ground outside of the hole looking in, with a clear unobstructed view of your client at the bottom of the hole, *sympathy* would be the act of climbing into the hole with the client and being "stuck" with the client. In contrast, a counselor displaying *empathy* would remain outside of the hole, maintaining the visual connection with the client the entire time and supporting the client to work at their own pace to navigate the current circumstance. The counselor *validates* the emotional, cognitive, and behavioral factors in this situation even though they are not able to directly relate because they are not "stuck in the hole." And, even if the counselor had previously been stuck in a hole themselves at one point in their life, it's not the same hole as this client's, and it's not the same experience as this client; therefore, the self-disclosure by the counselor may have a reverse or negative affect, especially because the counselor is not currently stuck. Regardless of whether you've ever been "stuck," showing awareness, acknowledging the thoughts and feelings expressed by the other person or group, and accepting all of this information as the truth for that person or group is how we can validate for others, even if we may not be able to relate. Validating is not mutually exclusive with agreeing. Each person has their own truth to speak and live. Supporting each other while we each do our best can be a powerful supportive experience.

- **Incoming transmission: Tell me more!** Invite open conversations that bring broad and inclusive perspectives to the group discussion. Many people communicate nonverbally more often than they do verbally. This can be even more complex when the communication is occurring in person or via a media that allows for both verbal and nonverbal communication to be happening simultaneously. Information overload! We have likely used the phrase "lost in translation" at one point in our life, referring to a direct experience we may have had or describing a situation someone else experienced. This phrase does not mean that there was a different language being used and a literal translation was misunderstood. You can probably recall an example of the same language being spoken and a misunderstanding still occurring. We are all so accustomed to the modern-day, fast-paced, instantaneous result that we risk skipping right by the opportunity for deeper meaning and understanding. Tone, intonation, context, and the combination of verbal and nonverbal communication can all have an impact on the messages being sent and received by people. As counselors, and in groups, we are able to adjust the dial on the speed of communications to intentionally and thoughtfully engage in interpersonal learning, listening, and understanding. This effort takes practice, especially because it requires each person to be actively present in ways that may be difficult to maintain in many cultures and systems. Actively listening to another person or a group does not mean agreement with all perspectives. It does mean that you are making the choice to be open to listening in nonjudgmental ways. It can take inner strength and courage to recognize that you do not know what you do not know about another person or a situation. Every individual will have their own unique life story that you will not know unless you take the time to actively listen and engage in open conversations with them.

- **Broach without battering.** Actively being a part of a group process will inevitably lead to new insights, thoughts, and questions. This will be true of your own inward reflections as well those of members of the group and the unique goals they have shared having. Whether engaged in a group experience or conversing with another person or group of people, keep in mind the motivations behind your comments or questions. More often than not, this insight can help you frame and focus questions or comments with a contextual lens that can make the receiver(s) less likely to feel that they are being "put on the hot seat," "put under a spotlight," or being "verbally attacked." Before broaching certain conversations and topics, look inward and ask yourself what comments or questions you might have and what might be your motivations behind these comments or questions. Perhaps the motivations are feelings of concern, love, hopefulness, or compassion. Perhaps the motivations are thoughts of self-shaming, doubt, or jealously, which would reflect more on the work that *you* need to do. Day Vines and colleagues (2007; 2013; 2018; 2020) have defined and developed and continue to provide evidence for the importance and impact of broaching behavior within individual counseling. Essentially, broaching behavior is a conceptual framework explicating how counselors have explicit discussions about racial, ethnic, and cultural factors with their clients during treatment. Particularly important is to open the door for all group members to feel safe to disclose but not be pestered, pressured, or obligated to do so. At times, members may feel pressure because their intersections of identity may imply that they are the "only" one or they are the "other" one. Broaching behavior is a powerful set of dispositions and language to invite members to be drawn in, yet battering members can foster oppressive environments especially if one is asked to disclose information to meet one's genuine curiosity.

- **Give "myvice" instead of advice.** The definition offered in Merriam-Webster dictionary for the noun *advice* is "a recommendation regarding a decision or course of conduct." Inherent in this is a sense of power. Common practice is the issuance of information that the receiver may either choose to accept and follow or to decline and not follow. Somehow our culture has become comfortable with this dichotomous output without seeking additional perspectives, critical thinking, or consideration of unique contextual factors that may be present. We recommend in group process and interpersonal communication an alternative approach that still invites the premise of the definition of the word, but shines more light on the *recommendation* part of the dictionary definition. To accomplish this, we have created our own word, *myvice*, acknowledging that what we will share and recommend is based our own unique perspective and on the information and understanding we have in that moment. Most important, through acknowledging our ownership of the perspective, we make intentional effort to remove the recommendation being delivered from a place of power and all-knowing truth. This shift in perspective actively invites the receiver to consider the recommendation and information, empowering them to still be the active decision maker versus accepting what we have shared as the decision being made for them. Following the guidance and direction of others remains an option, and in some cases, that may be the best decision a person can make. The point here is that we invite and empower the other person to make the call; rather than subtly (or not so subtly) imposing our own thoughts, values, experiences, biases, assumptions, and opinions on another person delivered as a recommendation. Myvice continues to share a unique perspective and thoughts from one person to another for a purpose of offering a different perspective or confirming a perspective another might be considering. Where we will see the most notable difference is with the inclusive and culturally responsive context that myvice will empower and invite.

Common Group Phases

Group phases are a helpful, concrete way to identify the specific point in the larger group process the group or group member(s) may be working through at a given time. Although group processes may be thought of as intervals or benchmarks reached, the proverbial distance and/or time it might take for individual members and the group as a whole to reach the different phases may or may not follow a specific pattern. Group leaders work to balance the rhythm and pace of the larger group based on the uniqueness of each member. Drawing out the therapeutic factors described above and focusing on the process (the experiences and feelings) versus the content supports this balance and flexibility.

Another strategy that assists group leaders, especially in the early stages as the members are learning the rhythm and process, is for the leader to keep the focus of the group on the "here and now" rather than to the "there and then." Often, when people think of counseling, they paint an image where the client spends the session exploring their past. Perhaps this is informed by the influence of a pioneer in the field, Dr. Sigmund Freud, whose approach to psychotherapy was oriented in events and experiences from the past, as far back as childhood, along with other unconscious thoughts and memories. Today, some argue that there are more than 400 theoretical approaches to assist counselors in a clinical practice, and they are not all grounded in a past-time orientation. For many group counseling experiences, especially those in a school setting, an approach that is focused on the present tense can be the most helpful for making meaning; adapting to shorter time-limited groups and sessions; and supporting cognitive, behavioral, and affective growth and development with a diverse group across many themes or topics. When group leaders refer to the "here and now," they are redirecting the attention and focus of the member(s) and the group to the present, current moment: "Right now, how does what just happened in the group make you feel?" Or, "what are your immediate thoughts?" Additionally, a leader may call attention to nonverbal behaviors that are actively playing out in reaction to an exchange that might invite meaning, insight, or interpersonal learning. A focus on the "there and then" may fit well within psychotherapy groups that are already structured for long-term and longer-duration sessions; however, this orientation is often not practical in a PreK-12 school setting. Regardless of which phase of group the leader and members may be navigating, these strategies will support the continued success and growth of the group process.

These popular stage approaches to classifying the evolution of the group process are adaptable to the four types of groups described earlier. Yalom (1995) identifies four stages: orientation or dependency, conflict or transition, cohesion, and termination. Corey et al. (2018) also offer a four-stage process: orientation/exploration, transition, working, consolidation and termination. Finally, Tuckman (1965) offers a five-stage approach: forming, storming, norming, performing, adjourning. Although the terms vary slightly, we can see within the semantics that all of these approaches clearly infuse a beginning, middle, and end to illustrate and represent the evolution of the group experience. Additionally, we can see that they clearly identify a point in the process where conflict (regarded as *transition* or *storming*) is an expected and desired concrete element within the evolution of the group experience.

During the prescreening and initial stages, group leaders may find it helpful to introduce, define, and discuss relevant key terms that may be important for the group process. This is especially recommended when the term(s) may also have a different meaning or understanding when used in a different context. For example, most individuals are likely to have a negative understanding or view of the term *conflict*. In modern society, *conflict* has almost become synonymous with aggression, violence, judgment, or narrow-mindedness. If a group member is not informed about how conflict in a group process can be a very different experience from that in the larger society, it is possible that when conflict occurs in the group (and it will, as part of the natural part of the group process) group members may engage in resistant behaviors, withdrawal from the process, or act out in the group in less productive or even maladaptive ways. Group leaders are constantly monitoring and addressing concerns they observe while simultaneously building the trust within the process and relationships and modeling giving and receiving feedback. These efforts pave the way for group members to monitor and address concerns they may observe directly as later stages of the group process are reached and the members assume more leadership in the process. Within groups, conflict is adaptive, inclusive, and invites purposeful and meaningful risk-taking for the goals of growth, learning, and development. We recognize that conflict has potential for positive feelings, thoughts, and behaviors in the group process. This is one example of the "power of group!" We also acknowledge the deep introspective and reflective work required in group processes that can be facilitated through conflict. In this way, conflict may still invite and create a sense of tension, uncomfortableness, or "thick air," as some members have referred to it.

Group dynamics and processes ebb and flow like the waves in the ocean. Groups are intentionally created and designed to be safe environments where risks, growth, and learning are possible. Building trust among members, leaders, and the group as a whole begins during the initial prescreening and is a critical component to foster and maintain throughout the entire group process to maximize outcomes. With trust in the group and the process, members are more likely to practice skills, behaviors, responses to situations, and more while they are in a group before trying the new and improved behavior, thoughts, or feelings in other environments or relationships.

Merriam-Webster defines *change* as "to make different or alter; to make radically different or transform; to give a different position, course or direction to; to replace with another; to make a shift from one to another or switch; and, to undergo a modification." Even the dictionary definition offers multiple perspectives, contextual considerations, and variables that may influence this powerful verb. It is no wonder how and why the act of *change* might be one of the most complex experiences individuals have; even though it can be argued we are constantly invited to experience change as a part of living. Change is inherent within the conflict process, and we all know that sometimes change is a smooth experience and that other times it is messy, messy, messy. Group leaders can help members during the early and formative stages of the group process to recognize and understand how conflict, within a group setting, can be the catalyst to reveal anxieties and invite insight and learning, guiding them on their change journey. However, a note of caution: if group leaders do not view conflict (or change) as a critical element within the process of the group they are leading, they may skip over this critical discussion at the beginning of the group process. This may create the possibility for maladaptive or negative conflict, as we might understand it in other situations outside of group, to occur.

It is incumbent upon leaders to recognize and meaningfully consider how conflict may manifest within the group they are leading, regardless of whether it is a task, psychoeducational, counseling/growth, or therapy group. It is easier to identify within the counseling/growth or therapy groups, because those take on a traditional group counseling approach. However, do not be misled! Conflict is still possible, and can still add significant value and purpose to the productivity, growth, and learning of the members and the group as a whole within task and psychoeducational groups. Most people want to be understood and want to understand what makes them special in this group (i.e., what value they bring). Conflict, even in a board meeting, as a popular task group example, will be a catalyst to helping each member and the group as a whole identify meaning, value, purpose, and direction to meet goals and outcomes effectively and efficiently.

Common Roles of Members Within Groups

The roles that group members assume often are a reflection of how the individual engages with others in their lives. Most often, the interpersonal behaviors observed especially within the beginning and working phases of the group process will reflect common elements of relationships with family members, friends, and, in some cases, close colleagues. It is possible that additional insights in the beginning phase may reflect slightly different behavior than the working phase, acknowledging that how individuals interact with strangers or acquaintances may be different. In general society, some may refer to this as the "different versions of oneself." Sometimes this provides permission or rationalization to either allow, dismiss, or judge thoughts, feelings, or behaviors. Part of the group experience can be to help each member see their true authentic self, and how their behaviors, thoughts, or feelings may vary based on other variables (e.g., environmental, situational, interpersonal), but in the end, their authentic self is there. The question then becomes, is the authentic self safe, protected, flourishing, and developing? If so, excellent! How can this continue to grow, maximizing strengths already in motion? If not, identifying and acknowledging that can be a hard first step. Now, looking to the future, how can the individual (with the support of the group) identify the pathway for meaningful change using clear goals as a support to guide the process?

Given the complexity of a group, it is possible that members may engage or drop out of a group in a manner atypical of behaviors in other interpersonal relationships if they have not been prepared for the group experience properly or there is an incompatibility, usually with the leader. Leaders often are able to observe signs in advance of the member taking any action. These observations may come as early as a prescreening interview or may be in any of the group sessions.

When completing a prescreening interview, leaders are attempting to assess several factors about the member and determine a goodness of fit based on the group purpose that has been identified. It is possible that a leader may determine that group counseling might benefit the potential member but that *this* specific group based on the topic or purpose is not a good match. Leaders may also observe personality, developmental, or behavioral characteristics that may not be a good fit with the group, such as low intrinsic motivation; poor communication, social, or self-disclosure skills; lack of insight or introspection; or a lack of awareness, interest, or motivation for any degree of change. Leaders may find it helpful to refer to the Johari window (Luft, 1984) as a way of classifying and understanding self-disclosure and interpersonal behavioral status.

Once a group has begun meeting, members may take on any one of the common roles often observed in a group. These roles are not formally assigned, and the member often has little to no awareness at the onset that they are assuming a role. Although this can be useful information for a leader, it can also be helpful to an individual member depending on what their goals are and what role they may be assuming. It is not uncommon for the role assumed, unconsciously, by a member to be associated with a goal for change the member has overtly shared with the group in the initial sessions. For example, a member of a counseling/growth or psychoeducational group might say that they want to work on not being an "advice-giver" all the time trying to solve everyone's problems, because they have received feedback from friends and family that it is negatively affecting their relationships. The member may even share that they feel other people pulling away or avoiding them because they "don't want advice," "they want their friend/family member," etc. In this type of scenario, the leader may observe this member taking on the attention-seeking role as an advice-giver. Their behaviors may even include an excess focus on others or monopolizing as a way to deflect engaging in their own personal growth work.

Several roles can be identified to help leaders conceptualize observed behaviors that may be known or unknown to the member at that time. For this reason, finding appropriate opportunities in group for leaders to engage members as well as model providing feedback will be critical to the larger process. The following are some of the more common behaviors commonly observed by counselors in the school setting:

- **Attention-seeking.** Attention-seeking behaviors often are employed as a way of deflecting from engaging in meaningful personal introspective work while still appearing to be actually engaging in the process. The intention of the behavior contrasted with the experience/outcome could be a powerful element to process in the group environment as a part of a working stage to affect all members and the group as a whole.

- **Blocking.** Blocking is a resisting behavior that impedes one's own progress or that of another group member or the group as a whole, such as refusing to participate in an activity or choosing to be silent in a distracting way. It is important to distinguish blocking by a member, which impedes the group growth process, from the blocking technique that a leader may employ that is an adaptive supportive technique to facilitate and continue growth, usually through an ambiguous or uncomfortable point in the discussion.
- **Monopolizing and manipulating.** These are two different behaviors, but they are similar in that they are an attempt to control others or the surrounding environment. Often, the impetus comes from anxieties or insecurities that are being triggered either by an individual or the environment. Leaders may be able to engage and model feedback to support growth and change if they observe patterns of a member engaging in these behaviors. This is an example of when patterns of behaviors in other relationships (friends, family, close coworkers) may be reflected in interpersonal and group relationships.
- **Encouraging.** These behaviors are often ones that may be assumed by leaders or members. Often, these are adaptive to a growth process in a supportive way to the goals, norms, or purpose of the group. It does not mean it will be "easy" or always comfortable, but positive outcomes evidenced in growth of members and/or group cohesion are more likely. Examples of encouraging behaviors might include gatekeeping that focuses on adherence to the norms and rules of the group; initiation where members take an intentional action towards a goal or growth for themself or a member; opinion or information-seeking will invite opportunities for interpersonal dialogue and interaction between members to learn and receive other perspectives; modeling and observation will often employ nonverbal communication, which is arguably the dominant type of communication we do in relationships, but it is not always acknowledged or discussed for its influence or impact.

Common Leadership Responsibilities for Groups

Leaders play a critical role in the group process even before the group meets for its first session. Common responsibilities of the group leader include, but are not limited to:

- Developing (and obtaining approval, as appropriate) a clear group theme and a plan to be able to concisely describe what and who the group is intended for
- Engaging in member screening interviews to determine goodness of fit based on the group theme and plan
- Providing members with a clear, yet big picture understanding of the group process, general expectations of the group roles, and anticipated goals and outcomes, along with other essential elements of informed consent appropriate to the type of group (this part will be more exhaustive for counseling/growth and therapy groups than it might for a task group)
- Describing and explaining the group structure and format (i.e., open or closed, timeline or duration)

Although the group leader will be able to meet and converse with each group member in advance as a part of the prescreening process, the group leader should keep in mind that the first session will be the first time the members are coming together as a group. This is critical, because based on the type of group and environment in which the group is occurring, some of the members may already know each other or have worked together. We see this especially within task and psychoeducational groups. This familiarity can be an advantage in some ways because it many allow the members and the group as a whole to progress through the initial stages of the group at a faster pace than a group with members who are meeting each other for the first time. The caution with this is that, regardless of prior knowledge, each group invites opportunities for new learning to occur at the intra- and interpersonal levels. Leaders are reminded to be clear and model this perspective so that members are not enabled to remain in the familiar and perhaps comfortable. Rather, invite, encourage, and engage for learning something new about yourself and someone else as there are always new things we can learn about a person even if we have known and worked with them for decades. This familiarity may also elicit the opposite response out of the gate if there are contentious or problematic stressors between members before they enter the group. Leaders must be cautioned in these cases and can often identify these frictions during the prescreening stage. Unless the group is designed to support and address these types of secondary, yet impactful, issues, it may not be as helpful to include both members at that time. Sometimes, there is not an option for a leader, and both or all members must be included. In this case, the prescreening sessions along with the initial sessions to establish group norms, rules, and expectations for interpersonal engagement will be essential. Leaders are reminded that the ultimate goal to strive for when leading a group is grounded in the *process*, not *perfection*.

There is an impetus to create a safe environment and group culture that invites productive conversations that support insight, learning, growth, and development among individual members and between members. Leaders strive to create the environment for group culture and cohesion to flourish. When the members of the group feel a sense of connectedness and belonging (as the hallmark of cohesion), they are typically more willing and likely to take risks themselves as well as to support others taking risks. Members are typically more willing to consider the perspectives of the other group members because they are invested and engaged in the overall process that has been created and formed by the members of this unique group. Cohesion, conflict, and a safe productive group environment are not easy to create and require intentional effort to maintain. They are essential to effective group work and the responsibility of the leader to strive for these goals. See the box for more information on leadership skills that are essential for the group leader/facilitator.

ESSENTIAL LEADERSHIP SKILLS FOR GROUP COUNSELING INTERVENTIONS

Note that these skills are typically included in graduate-level group counseling, but there is some transferability to supporting group work processes even when the group is not a traditional counseling intervention. Some of the following leadership skills have similar terms and overlapping definitions with other key terms or therapeutic factors described earlier in this chapter.

- Reflection of feelings
- Knowledgeable goals

- Silence
- Validation
- Cultural relevance
- Give clients what they need
- Refrain from judgment
- Guide without leading conversation
- Slow down
- Active listening
- Linking
- Teaching or coaching
- Listening
- Humor
- Blocking
- Self-disclosure
- Questioning
- Reflection of content
- Confrontation
- Asset building/encouragement
- Immediacy
- Integration of culture and other aspects of identity
- Giving and receiving feedback

Communication, Consultation, and Collaboration

School counselors have great communication skills. These skills apply well in individual sessions (e.g., one-on-one interactions) that could include a counselor and a teacher, a counselor and a parent, or a counselor and a student, just to name a few. School counselors can also apply these communication skills in group settings that include group counseling interventions, programs, and other meetings. In addition to communication skills, which can be summed up as intentional listening, contextualizing what has been heard, giving and receiving feedback, and concentrating on areas to improve upon in future encounters, school counselors can also serve as consultants to others. In the role of consultant, the school counselor is hearing one or more individuals' concerns and offering suggestions on how to tackle these problems with solutions that are reasonable, feasible, and effective. The consultant role present within a group setting is more complex because there are more players to contend with. There are also likely more stakeholders that the group is concerned about. Applying the principles outlined in this text can help with fulfilling a consultant role for groups of individuals.

Collaboration is another skill that is discussed as part of a school counselor's training and preparation program. *Collaboration* can be defined as the process of two or more people working in concert to accomplish something successfully (Baker et al., 2009). More specifically, Baker and colleagues expand the definition of collaboration to suggest that both parties mutually seek ways to understand and address conflicts or challenges. Intentional steps to addressing conflicts include engaging in identifying options to address the problem. First; the problem is defined, then solutions are identified, all viable solutions are explored, additional information is considered, and then the most appealing solution is chosen. After the implementation of the options, outcomes are evaluated and additional options are generated as needed (Baker et al., 2009). Collaboration coupled with effective communication continues to be an essential characteristic of a school counselor (Young & Kaffenberger, 2015).

A school counselor is charged to collaborate with all of the same stakeholders with whom they might facilitate the groups mentioned in this chapter. Collaboration is highlighted because it offers the connotation that there is no expert in the equation, but rather all parties involved are instrumental in the overall success of the mission. Furthermore, collaboration is successful when individuals fulfill roles based in part on their unique skill sets. Collaboration is not an equal process, but rather an equitable process in that all members of the collaborative team have unique needs and distinct talents, and within the right environment these needs and talents can be matched to accomplish the goals set forth. The potential for impact of effective and intentional collaboration is not only on the parties who are directly involved; collaboration can affect systems and change cultures (Bemak, 2000). This is also a common outcome of intentional and healthy group dynamics.

More important, when it comes to group counseling interventions school counselors will more often run psychoeducational groups, because they are better designed for work in a school setting and are more developmentally appropriate for the children and adolescents they will work with (Erford, 2010). Because of this reality in the field, and the gap between what is taught during their preservice education and what school counselors will actually deal with concerning children, adolescents, and other adults they may interface with in a school setting, the majority of school counseling training programs do not incorporate group work from any other perspective to assist with training, professional identity development, or broadening the preservice school counselor's skill sets.

Pulling It All Together

Group counseling and group work shares similarities with individual counseling. We can observe similar techniques, skills, and conceptualizations informed by theories or frameworks in many ways. However, despite these overlapping similarities to a professional helping role and the counseling process focused on growth, introspective learning, and adaptive change, the paradigm and delivery of group work and group counseling has its own unique terms, skills, and framework to guide and inform clinical best practice that is both ethical and inclusive of a diverse membership.

We discussed the four common types of groups as defined by the ASGW, noting that not all may be appropriate in a school setting. We explored different purposes, influences, and considerations a leader must factor in planning and preparing for a group. We identified some of the common roles members may have and skills a leader may likely need to employ in a group process. In the upcoming chapters, we will use these terms and concepts as we demonstrate the application and versatility of group work within the school setting.

DISCUSSION QUESTIONS

1. At this point, how would you define *group counseling*? How would you define *group work*? If you were to expand your definition of group counseling to group work in school settings, what would that look like?

2. What types of groups have you experienced or observed in the school?

3. Which of the therapeutic factors seem most applicable to you when you think about the types of groups you often experience or observe in the school?

4. As you consider the common roles of group members, do any of them resonate with you as "familiar" in that you or someone you know may have illustrated a characteristic described? Are there roles that you know might be harder for you to work with than others?

5. As you consider some of the common responsibilities of a leader, what personal strengths come to mind as part of your skill set or knowledge base? Are there areas that may benefit from continued education or additional training?

REFERENCES

Baker, S. B., Robichaud, T. A., Dietrich, V. C. W., Wells, S. C., & Schreck, R. E. (2009). School counselor consultation: A pathway to advocacy, collaboration, and leadership. *Professional School Counseling, 12*(3), 200–206. https://doi.org/10.1177/2156759X0901200301

Bemak, F. (2000). Transforming the role of the counselor to provide leadership in education reform through collaboration. *Professional School Counseling, 3*(5), 323.

Broderick, P. C., & Blewitt, P. (2020). *The life span: Human development for helping professionals* (5th ed.). Pearson.

Corey, M. S., Corey, G., & Corey, C. (2018). *Groups: Process and practice* (10th ed.). Cengage.

Day-Vines, N. L., Booker Ammah, B., Steen, S., & Arnold, K. M. (2018). Getting comfortable with discomfort: Preparing counselor trainees to broach racial, ethnic, and cultural factors with clients during counseling. *International Journal for the Advancement of Counselling, 40*, 89–104. https://doi.org/10.1007/s10447-017-9308-9

Day-Vines, N. L., Bryan, J., & Griffin, D. (2013). The Broaching Attitudes and Behavior Survey (BABS): An exploratory assessment of its dimensionality. *Journal of Multicultural Counseling and Development, 41*, 210–223. https://doi.org/10.1002/j.2161-1912.2013.00037.x

Day-Vines, N. L., Cluxton-Keller, F., Agorsor, C., Gubara, S., & Otabil, N. A. A. (2020). The multidimensional model of broaching behavior. *Journal of Counseling and Development, 98*, 107–118. https://doi.org/10.1002/jcad.12304

Day-Vines, N. L., Wood, S. M., Grothaus, T., Craigen, L., Holman, A., Dotson-Blake, K., & Douglass, M. J. (2007). Broaching the subjects of race, ethnicity, and culture during the counseling process. *Journal of Counseling and Development, 85*, 401–409. https://doi. org/10.1002/j.1556-6678.2007.tb00608.x

DeLucia-Waack, J. L. (2006). *Leading psychoeducational groups for children and adolescents.* SAGE Publications.

Erford, B. T. (2010). *Group work in the schools.* Pearson.

Gladding, S. T. (2019). *Groups: A counseling specialty* (8th ed.). Pearson.

Luft, J. (1984). *Group processes: An introduction to group dynamics* (3rd ed.). Mayfield Publishing.

Meier, S. T., & Davis, S. R. (2019). *The elements of counseling* (8th ed). Waveland Press, Inc.

Tuckman, B. W. (1965). Developmental sequence in small groups. *Psychological Bulletin, 63*(6), 384–399. https://doi.org/10.1037/h0022100

Yalom, I. D. (1995). *The theory and practice of group psychotherapy* (4th ed.). Basic Books.

Yalom, I. D. (2005). *The theory and practice of group psychotherapy* (5th ed.). Basic Books.

Yalom, I. D., & Leszcz, M. (2020). *The theory and practice of group psychotherapy* (6th ed). Basic Books.

Young, A., & Kaffenberger, C. (2015). School counseling professional development: Assessing the use of data to inform school counseling services. *Professional School Counseling, 19*(1), 1096–2409. https://doi.org/10.5330/1096-2409-19.1.46

Prepare and Apply the TRATE My Group Framework in PreK-12 Public Schools

PreK-12 school buildings are microsystems representing the communities and populations they serve. Even in communities and geographic locations that may appear to be mostly homogenous on a variety of demographic variables, public schools are complex systems with diverse and unique individuals. Given this, public schools can be an ideal location to effectively and efficiently utilize group work techniques and knowledge to facilitate and support interpersonal relationships, communications, and cultural awareness from a young age to influence and inform all ages. We can learn and grow as individuals through active engagement in an intentional group process. We can build on our strengths, practice and enhance our areas of development, and share our learning with others as we learn from them as well. Groups are dynamic opportunities for intra- and interpersonal learning for individuals of all ages, backgrounds, and goals.

Consider the former NBC motto that once chimed during commercials, "The More You Know" with the three notes of a xylophone in the background. Acknowledging that the goal is to be mindful of the culture and environment required to foster and invite the dynamic intra- and interpersonal learning described above, the TRATE My Group framework considers multiple perspectives, stake-holders, and variables to proactively set the group leader and its members up for success.

Our society has become so fast-paced and emotionally reactive that unbiased knowledge and comprehensive understanding that accounts for multiple perspectives is rarely a priority today with regard to communication. We also see this in schools when we observe students interacting with each other via technology, social media, and abbreviated posts that may limit communication by encouraging or requiring pictures instead of complete thoughts or restricting character length that limits the length of comments, increasing chances for misunderstandings or misinterpreta-tion. Many of the communication platforms used by students are also asynchronous, meaning that live, in-person, real-time conversation is not occurring. The immediate effect of words is not experienced, and nonverbal communication is not possible to add context and meaning to the words being shared. This can create challenges for intra- and interpersonal development among children and adolescents. We also observe communication concerns with students relying on emojis or slang rather than engaging in self-reflection to identify (to the best of their developmental abilities) their feelings, thoughts, and behaviors and to work to communicate those in respectful ways using complete thoughts, sentences, or questions. The larger issue of reduced focus on critical thinking, reflective thinking, and autonomous learning in PreK-12 schools has been a hot topic of conversation for decades in the United States. This is not surprising when we consider that school curriculums, as stated in state legislation or state board of education policies in many states, have removed requirements for grammar, English composition and writing, critical thinking, economics sequences, financial and business planning sequences, and overall critical thinking. In many states, cursive is no longer taught in elementary schools, such that today many children and adolescents do not know how to sign their name. The broader societal norms that influence and inform common communication behaviors among children and adolescents are important to consider when preparing and planning for facilitating a group that will be made up of children and adolescents.

Similarly, it is also important to consider the variables and context that may be influencing and informing the adults in the school building, including teachers, administrators, counselors, and staff. The influences coming from outside of the physical school building, such as directives and requirements from central/district offices, state departments of education, and the U.S. Department of education, are profound.

One example of a variable we have observed as having an impact on adults in schools is that of high-stakes testing. In many schools throughout the country, high-stakes tests are administered at the end of each year or on a 2- or 3-year cycle. Testing schedules may be informed by grade level or by building level, often determined by requirements from the state department of education. State-mandated tests are administered at multiple levels, often with second or third grade being an initial benchmark. The College Board, the American College Testing (ACT) program, and the Educational Testing Service (ETS) are three popular third-party organizations that serve PreK-12 and higher education institutions in managing and administering high-stakes testing options. The College Board administers the SAT and PSAT; ACT administers its namesake exam. The SAT, PSAT, and ACT are used to assess high school students for college readiness. Many colleges and universities use SAT or ACT results as part of their admissions requirements for students who seek to matriculate at their institutions. Interestingly, this requirement is increasingly becoming a topic of conversation and debate with regards to the ability of these tests to accurately assess for college readiness and whether they are accessible for all students who may have postsecondary educational goals. The ETS is known for its high-stakes tests that are taken by students who have already matriculated to a college or university. It offers exams such as the PRAXIS, which measures the academic skills and subject-specific content knowledge needed for careers in education. Many states require the PRAXIS as part of obtaining education licenses for employment in the field. The ETS also administers the Graduate Record Exam (GRE), a commonly used entrance exam for graduate school, and, the Test of English as a Foreign Language (TOEFL), which assesses English-language proficiency and is often required for nonnative speakers who wish to attend English-speaking universities.

Part of what seems to be influencing the adults in the school buildings around the outcomes of these high-stakes tests and other requirements is the direct financial implication of the test results. Salaries, bonuses, and district funding are more enmeshed with third-party testing outcomes than ever before. In addition, the tense political climate throughout the country also influences the public school culture. We invite you to consider some of the local implications by the political climate on your public school environment. As we consider these additional pressures faced by the adults in the schools, being able to pull students out of classes to engage in a group experience becomes increasingly difficult. Sadly, this is true even if the group outcomes are expected to have a direct effect of supporting the academic skills and aptitude that are assessed on these high-stakes tests. It is important to acknowledge the pressure and potential negative distracting influence these high-stakes tests may have on the larger school climate and culture. Today, schools are less focused on comprehensive learning and growth to be a knowledgeable citizen of the world and more focused on teaching content that will be specifically assessed on an upcoming test so that the different stakeholders involved receive their respective rewards (e.g., the student achieving a score to advance to the next level; the teacher receiving a bonus; the administration/building/district obtaining additional funding from the state; the state having data to showcase effective educational outcomes within their state to the federal government, which can also influence access to monies or opportunities for future monies). Planning and delivery of group-based prevention and intervention in a school will be complex, but do not shy away, because the opportunity for impact on all levels of the system is profound!

The plethora of inequalities faced by most people, overt or covert, will manifest within the public school culture. Importantly, school counselors and other adults within the school building can offer opportunities to thoughtfully engage in meaningful, adaptive, respectful, and growth-based learning. Schools are a terrific starting place to influence multiple generations and to build and practice new norms that affect cultures and communities. So, how do we begin this important work? How do we get buy-in from all of the stakeholders? How do we begin to make changes to a larger system? Great questions! Let's begin with counselors preparing themselves for a facilitator/leader role to plan for and advocate for the importance of groups in their schools. The TRATE My Group framework is designed to address all of these variables and support effective and efficient best practice of the school counselor. Prepared counselors are in the best position to adapt to meet the evolving complexities inherent in group environments.

Foundational Knowledge, Contextual Dimensions, and Practice

The objectives for this chapter build on the knowledge obtained in earlier chapters and prepare counselors for practical application of the TRATE My Group framework. Across specializations and delivery approaches, counselors prepare for intentional and meaningful work with their clients. Although the TRATE My Group framework can be easily adapted to support the work of other clinical counseling specializations or nonclinical settings outside of a traditional school building, the framework has been designed to address the unique complexities that are inherent to the public PreK-12 school setting in the United States. This chapter will address the following three areas that apply most directly to preparation for applying the TRATE My Group framework:

1. Group leadership and communication styles
2. Self-care, wellness, and balance strategies
3. Intersectionality of culturally diverse clients and self-awareness

An overarching goal of the TRATE My Group framework is grounded in supporting efficient and effective best counselor practices. To that end, preparation steps that include ongoing self-reflection can occur prior to implementing the TRATE My Group framework to amplify this desired goal. Let's discuss each step individually before exploring how these areas are in constant motion as a part of this dynamic framework focused on efficient and effective best practice for counselors.

Preparation Step 1: Group Leadership and Communication Styles

This first step can also be completed as a part of a discussion in clinical supervision if the counselor is engaged in an active supervisory relationship. It can also be a part of a collegial conversation among peers, different from clinical supervision, such as set regional counselor groups or director groups. It is widely accepted that one of the most essential skills for a professional counselor (regardless of specialization) is communication. For some, it may appear effortless as they navigate conversations with a client or a group, being able to attend to individuals and facilitate the counseling process. Communication is assuredly a highly practiced skill that has been crafted and fine-tuned throughout the counselor's career with intentionality, active engagement and purposeful risk-taking and an openness to the learning, growth, and development processes. Interestingly, these are often general expectations for clients or group members.

Counselors learn and apply throughout their professional training a variety of leadership and communication microskills that build the foundation of their practice. These include interpersonal, intrapersonal, listening, analysis, and communication skills. Empathetic reflective practice is a cornerstone of these microskills. This invites the counselor to be fully attentive to the client or group members in the counseling process that is occurring, balanced with allowing the client or group members to be in a safe space, inviting an authentic experience. Whether it is individual counseling or group counseling, a general assumption is that the reason for the action is to support or guide some form of growth, change, awareness, or development. Although there are several positives to this broad-strokes goal, it is important to remember that change is a process, and that for some people, it is a very difficult process.

Factors such as personality, temperament, and developmental level may all play profound roles in the communication, interpersonal, and/or leadership style that an individual brings to the process. Furthermore, depending on these traits and characteristics of the individual, if they are less adaptive to the goals of the group (e.g., a personality commonly resistant and passive to change, who is tasked to lead a task group with direct concrete goals for change), there may be additional levels of challenge.

Before a counselor begins leading a group, they are invited to continuously reflect on their own leadership, communication, and conflict-resolution styles. Each individual has strengths and contributions to offer as a group leader, and one intention of the TRATE My Group framework is to support efficient and effective application of key elements embedded in group counseling and group work to aid in this effort. Knowing yourself is a critical first step to being an effective counselor and an effective group leader!

GROUPS IN ACTION

What Is Your Most Common Leadership Style?

One of the most efficient ways for individuals today to initiate self-reflection is by completing a focused quiz intended to provide meaningful insight about the individual's thoughts, feelings, or behaviors. An ever-growing number of quizzes are available online to aid a diverse labor market interested and impacted by leadership-style awareness, growth, and development. In the 1930s, psychologist Dr. Kurt Lewin focused his scholarly work on designing a model of leadership styles. He identified three core leadership styles: (1) authoritarian (autocratic), (2) participative (democratic), and, (3) delegative (laissez-faire). Variations of his model in paid and free versions are accessible on the Internet. Here are a few examples:

- Dr. Kurt Lewin's Leadership Style Quiz (free; adapted): https://www.mindtools.com/pages/article/leadership-style-quiz.htm
- Leadership Style Quiz (handout; adapted and expanded from Dr. Lewin's model): https://www.paproviders.org/archives/Pages/Conference_Archive_2014/handouts/W46_Shanahan_Leadership_Style_Quiz.pdf
- True Colors Personality Quiz: https://wedgworthleadership.com/wp-content/uploads/2016/08/True-Colors-Personality-Quiz.pdf
- Four Personality Types with Animal Representations: http://nealybrown.com/wp-content/uploads/2013/09/Four-Personality-Types1.pdf

What Is Your Most Common Communication Style?

Similar to leadership-style quizzes, there are several communication-style quizzes. Although there may be less variance among professional counselors with regard to communication styles as compared to leadership styles, we intentionally invite this active area of self-reflection as part of the ongoing development and awareness process. Additionally, the TRATE My Group framework will invite collaboration and involvement with a diverse group of stakeholders internal and external to the school. Awareness and knowledge about communication styles is just as important for an individual counselor as it is to have an understanding about the types of communication styles they may be receiving from others who are in their group. As a group leader or a group member, this knowledge and awareness can contribute to the overall group culture and inclusion, especially if members or the process reach an impasse.

A number of models of communication styles have been developed. Dr. David Merrill was a key contributor to identifying specific communication styles. His framework identified four styles: (1) driver, (2) expressive, (3) amiable, and (4) analytical. Dr. Tony Alessandra developed a model with four terms that blends work from Dr. Carl Jung's personality types and Hippocrates four temperaments to create four communication styles: (1) analyzer, (2) director, (3) socializer, and (4) relator. A third example is the four communication styles developed by entrepreneur and consultant Mark

Murphy: (1) analytical, (2) functional, (3) intuitive, and (4) personal. These models have been adapted to several free and paid online versions of quizzes accessible to the public. Examples include:

- Five Main Communication Style Quiz: https://www.glassdoor.com/blog/quiz-whats-your-communication-style/
- Dr. Merrill's Communication Style Quiz: https://static1.squarespace.com/static/5c412ab755b-02cec3b4ed998/t/5c9a7f44f9619a5697aa7f01/1553628996672/Communication+Exercise+-March2019.pdf
- Dr. Alessandra's Communication Style Quiz: https://visme.co/blog/the-4-communication-styles-quiz/
- Murphy's Communication Style Quiz: https://www.leadershipiq.com/blogs/leadership-iq/39841409-quiz-whats-your-communication-style

Preparation Step 2: Self-Care, Wellness, and Balance Strategies

Regardless of how long you have been practicing in the field, active and ongoing self-care, wellness, and healthy balance strategies are critical for a counselor and helping professional. We are offered this reminder by the airlines anytime we fly on an airplane: "One must first put their own oxygen mask on before helping others." The same is true for counselors. What are your strategies for monitoring your wellness, and how do you ensure that your arsenal of strategies to help you revive, reset, and renew are meeting your current needs?

The need for self-care, wellness, and balance strategies has become a prominent topic of discussion throughout specializations in the field. Professional development, research, and skills built into clinical training as a part of graduate school have become common and essential. Even still, many counselors still need to be actively reminded to take time for their own self-care.

Research has shown that the working relationship between a counselor and their students/client(s) is one of the most impactful predictors for achieving successful counseling outcomes (Bryan et al., 2011; Tang & Ng, 2019). In order for counselors to lay the foundation for these strong relationships to grow and form, the counselor must be in a healthy and grounded place to do this essential work. Being innately empathetic or a helper does not automatically make someone impervious to stress, exhaustion, emotional depletion, and burnout. One of the most challenging pieces about monitoring self-care, wellness, and burnout status is that it can be hard to gauge, because even when dealing with complex and difficult situations counselors engaged in the work can feel validated and positive because of the direct impact they are having to effect a change for the better. Hard, exhausting, ambiguous, and/or challenging work can be incredibly rewarding, and counselors are certainly among those who experience this paradox on a regular basis.

There is no doubt that school counselors add value to the PreK-12 school setting in a myriad of ways with regard to prevention and intervention. There are endless examples of the unique versatility of this essential and critical support role within the school building. As a resource for students, parents, and adults in the building, school counselors are able to adapt to practically every need that could arise in a school day. It is no wonder that this field continues to struggle with issues around role ambiguity and role confusion within itself as well as in the professional field; the versatility of the school counselor is profound.

School counselors will adapt and transform to the immediate and sequential needs of each situation by intentionally assessing situations, prioritizing risks, ensuring safety, and maintaining a safe school culture and environment for all and executing interventions as appropriate to the situation, collaborating and consulting with others as needed. We acknowledge and appreciate that school counselors wear and transition a variety of "hats" daily—this is simply "business as usual." We also recognize that working at this high level of intensity can be problematic for the counselor. This is especially true when the breadth and depth of work (on a daily basis nonetheless) is often minimized or in some instances not recognized at all due in part to larger systemic challenges of role ambiguity that have been ongoing for decades. *Burnout, wellness,* and *balance* are all key terms that have provided a spotlight for discussion and continuing education in recent years for the counseling field as a whole. School counselors are no exception.

GROUPS IN ACTION

Self-Care, Wellness, and Balance Self-Reflection Activity

Reflect on the past 48 hours, the past 7 days, the past 2 weeks, and the past month as you consider the following self-reflection questions:

- Catalog your primary actions, activities, and behaviors over the timeframe chosen. What patterns do you see? What appears to be a priority? Does this shift the balance you thought you had or want at this time and moving forward?

- Catalog the primary thoughts and feelings you've had toward yourself over the timeframe chosen. What patterns do you see? What recurring messages do you seem to be telling yourself? What feelings appear to have a significant presence? Do your responses to these questions empower your inner sense of purpose, balance, and confidence as a unique individual?

- Catalog the primary thoughts and feelings you've had about others (i.e., family, friends, and/or strangers) over the timeframe chosen. What patterns do you see? What assumptions or generalizations are apparent? What feelings appear to have a significant presence? Do your responses to these questions empower healthy and adaptive interpersonal relationships and collaborations?

- If you could try something new this week to work toward achieving a greater sense of balance, what would it be? How would you know if it worked? What change(s) do you expect within yourself?

Meditation Apps Available for Smartphones or Mobile Devices

1. Calm
2. Aware
3. Headspace
4. Mesmerize
5. Insight Timer
6. Breathe
7. MyLife Meditation
8. BetterMe
9. Meditation Nest
10. Mindfulness
11. Simple Habit Sleep
12. Sattva
13. Daily Meditation
14. Deep Meditation
15. Prana Breath
16. Stop, Breathe, & Think
17. Sanvello (formerly Pacifica)
18. Let's Meditate

Preparation Step 3: Cultural and Diversity Awareness

We recognize and acknowledge these areas as a part of ongoing development and growth of one's understanding, perspectives, knowledge, biases, assumptions, beliefs, values, prejudices, and related "-isms." In our culturally diverse society, intersectionalities of cultures, customs, practices, and perspectives are a rich part of our daily lives. This is especially true in many communities throughout the United States. Each individual's level of awareness, understanding, and acceptance may be different. Many of the central aspects that comprise each individual's identity are not overt or visible. And, some that are visible may have different meanings or representations.

A challenge is that although societal norms are adapting and expanding to acknowledge the complexities and depth of elements that comprise one's identity, they also are hindered by an overall reactive, impulsive, emotionally charged perspective. Courageous conversations are being more frequently encouraged; however, not all communities and systems have established a foundation to respectfully, safely, and civilly invite people to engage in this discourse to learn, share, and grow. This is illustrated every day within the PreK-12 schools because they are microsystems of the communities around them. School personnel have an increased responsibility to be aware of their inherent power and privileges as educators. Acknowledging the purpose for relationships between adults in the school building and the stakeholders served (e.g., students, parents, external stakeholders) may help prepare the counselor to facilitate (as a group leader) or engage (as a group member) adaptive interpersonal communication.

Ultimately, a broad-sweeping challenge and opportunity counselors will have is to model, support, facilitate, and advocate for slowing down the processes so that complete communication and context can be thoughtfully considered versus rushing and sacrificing a meaningful dialogue. Too often, when emotions dominate a conversation or exchange between two or more individuals, it is the emotional interpretation that stays with the parties involved after the conversation ends. The content and important points, even if they are grounded in a subjective perspective, may be "lost" in the overwhelming emotionally charged exchange. Engaging in challenging conversations is needed, absolutely. We can all enhance and grow by learning from others, considering perspectives different than our own, and challenging ourselves to think, act, and embrace uniqueness. This system-level macro change cannot occur overnight, regardless of how frequent or loud the call may be. The invitation extended is complex, and has the potential to impact and influence all layers of our complex selves and systems. Recognizing that this is a natural element in communication outside of a counseling setting, we can see how essential this preparation skill is to preparing a group leader for success when they are in the group experience because these will be expected continued behaviors in group as well that will require leaders to facilitate and direct toward adaptive solutions so that members can strive for insights and meaning.

GROUPS IN ACTION

The Big Invitation of the Century

Will you accept the following invitation? How will you extend the invitation to others you know (e.g., friends, family, coworkers, neighbors)? How will you extend the invitation to strangers?

As an important member of this group, system, community, culture, society, and country, you are cordially invited to …

- Be patient with yourself and with others.
- Show kindness to others, even if they may knowingly or unknowingly offended or insulted your identity or sense of self in some way.
- Respond balancing authentic emotions in the here-and-now while actively increasing the use of adaptive communication to help inform, education, and encourage awareness or understanding of things/perspectives that may be different.
- Love and respect yourself first, and let that shine for others to see versus expecting others to first love and respect you.
- Trust yourself, because you know yourself better than any other person on the planet. And if you don't, then take the time to get to know yourself, because there is a spectacular person waiting to meet you!
- Accept that although you have your own unique "awesomeness," you are human. Mistakes, setbacks, and challenges are all opportunities in disguise! Do not pass up opportunities for growth.

Consistent with historical trends, a majority of the adults in public PreK-12 school buildings throughout many areas of the United States are White, and many are women. It is important to acknowledge that there is implicit inequality that has a significant effect on many students and adults in schools and communities throughout the United States. This may be illustrated by racial inequalities, access inequalities, gender or age inequalities, and so much more. How can we acknowledge, consider, and respect (regardless of whether we appreciate or value) the differences in each person we work with directly and as a part of a group in more considerate, safe, and equitable ways? And, when we do not like something that someone has done or said, how can we call upon our interpersonal and communication skills to engage in more adaptive, knowledge-based, versus opinion-based, conversations with an underlying goal of learning and growth for all involved? For many children and adolescents, this interpersonal skill set is significantly aided when they observe adults who they feel "look like them" or can better relate to their life experiences to date. In addition to educating and fulfilling their respective responsibilities for their jobs each day in school, all adults in the school serve as vital role models for the students, whether they are aware of it or not. Business and marketing fields have capitalized on advertising and promotional campaigns that are centered on making the consumer feel connected to the spokesperson or message to sell their product. Subliminal reinforcement confirming "yes, that person (or people) understand me" is a powerful key to unlocking opportunities for thoughts, feelings, behaviors, and understanding. We can apply these principles in a school setting through our work by acknowledging the cultural implications within the school system and among the student as well as adult populations in the schools. Awareness and acknowledgement is always a good starting point to effect change and invite culturally aware and inclusive practices and dialogues.

Engaging in complex, exhausting (yet crucial) diversity- and social justice–focused advocacy work often takes an unprecedented amount of energy. It can be profoundly rewarding, as well as shockingly disappointing. We all bring unique stories, perspectives, and contributions to the larger table. One next step we can all take together is to expand the invitation to consider each person's uniqueness. This requires everyone to be open to sharing their perspective in respectful and constructive ways, recognizing that some listeners may be hearing a particular perspective for the first time. It is not about agreeing or disagreeing or winning arguments or debates. Rather, it is about a willingness to engage in a civil discourse with a fellow human being with a shared interest grounded in knowledge, learning, and a sense of togetherness. Adults need to model what this looks like for the children and adolescents to help guide the next generations to achieve and strive for more than the generations that came before them. Outcomes from a civil discourse such as this may include all parties involved affirming that their perspective rings true for them; but, what will be different, is that they will now have expanded their awareness about themselves for *why* their perspective resonates with them and will have listened to and considered other perspectives as well. As we think of the PreK-12 school setting and several groups, especially task groups, this approach can be especially helpful.

As illustrated by several events at the local, state, and national levels throughout history, we can see an underlying theme of racism, privilege, and inequalities. Almost every person can identify a personal example from their lives where they have experienced an injustice, bias, or prejudice. Despite this, stating that we live and/or work in racist or unjust environments appears to spark immediate defensive reactions, hostility, and divisiveness. The "us versus them" or "me versus you" power imbalance often has an immediate impact. Let's be clear—this is not isolated to race or ethnicity either. Examples include, but are not limited to:

- Gender
- Sex
- Language (speaking, reading, and writing, as well as strength of other accents when speaking in English)
- Nonverbal behaviors and communications
- Education completed (high school; GED; postsecondary education at a 2-year, 4-year, public, private, or vocational institution)
- Location (geographic or specific institutions) of where education or postsecondary education was earned
- Military service (branch, role/rank while in service, discharge status)
- Marital status
- If someone has children or not, including how those children behave and/or their abilities and capabilities
- Mental health issues of the individual or a family member (diagnosed or undiagnosed, known or unknown)
- Socioeconomic status of an individual or family
- Technological skills and knowledge of and access to technologies

A resource for supporting counselors' efforts to engage in inclusive and competent practices is the Multicultural Counseling Competencies guide developed and authored by the Association for Multicultural Counseling and Development (AMCD), a division of the American Counseling Association (ACA). This guide is available at https://www.counseling.org/resources/competencies/multcultural_competencies.pdf.

Groups, by their very nature, are a platform to engage with multiple people who inherently will have similarities and differences. How can we most effectively balance the goals of the group with the possible challenges that some or all of the members may also be navigating? Our suggestion is to focus on the intersectionality of three essential pillars that can, together, create a powerful group experience that is productive and invites civil engagement of all. The first pillar balances the *authentic inclusion* of the variety of perspectives and voices of the members in the group. The second pillar attends to creating and maintaining a *safe and productive group or work environment* necessary for the goals of the group. The third pillar acknowledges that we do not know everything about a person's journey and experiences, and thus we recognize that the *diverse perspectives* of some (or all) members in the group may include experiences with oppression, marginalization, or injustice. This third pillar is not an excuse, minimization, or dismissal of the member(s) fulfilling their identified responsibilities and expectations as a part of the group. Instead, it is an accepted awareness intended to establish and grow safe and inclusive environments that foster antiracist and trauma-sensitive climates. These pillars seek to bridge the gap and provide access for all who are interested and willing to choose to be a part of this way of engaging with others.

Let's consider the invitation extended and work to slow the processes within various systems and communities to invite conversation driven by knowledge versus reactions driven by emotional impulse. Let's consider the invitation extended and work on intrapersonal growth, love, and acceptance as the first priority so that you may model as well as speak your truth from your heart from a calm and secure sense of self and not demand instantaneous respect and acceptance with combative contention (especially from strangers). Let's consider the invitation to be flexible and adaptable to a changing community, society, and country as an opportunity versus dismissing, ignoring, or retaliating to resist change and growth of any form. By using the TRATE My Group framework, opportunities to engage in these critical perspectives and work will be plentiful for group leaders and members.

GROUPS IN ACTION

Several free self-assessments are available to support the active self-reflection process to identify and recognize where an individual may be on the spectrum of acceptance, tolerance, and/or understanding with cultural differences:

- American Speech-Language-Hearing Association checklist: https://www.asha.org/siteassets/uploadedfiles/Cultural-Competence-Checklist-Personal-Reflection.pdf
- Central Vancouver Island Multicultural Society checklist: http://www.coloradoedinitiative.org/wp-content/uploads/2015/10/cultural-competence-self-assessment-checklist.pdf
- Cultural Competence Self-Awareness checklist (author unknown): https://emamtsaderis.files.wordpress.com/2016/11/awareness_self_assessment-copy.pdf
- National Center for Cultural Competence at Georgetown University: https://nccc.georgetown.edu/curricula/assessment/index.html

---

The TRATE My Group Framework

Purposeful exploration of group counseling leadership and related skills applicable in a school setting is critical, especially because the preparation during a master's program is narrowly focused to clinical settings, often serving an adult or older adolescent population, and lacks a broad application to the school setting (Vannatta & Steen, 2019). We refresh the fundamental knowledge and skills gleaned from training and inform those in other roles who have not yet learned this subject matter knowledge. The prior knowledge, assumptions, experiences or ideas that you have will build on the TRATE mnemonic to inform efficient and best practices for a myriad of group work opportunities within the school setting and school community.

The TRATE My Group framework allows group leaders to have a clear and intentional understanding of what type of group they are leading *and* how they can be most effective and efficient in their role as a group leader. A group member may also consider applying this framework to enhance insights and perspectives from the member lens, although that is optional. This framework provides guidance to leaders, and by extension, every member participating in any type of group.

The framework helps to identify and consider the following elements that have a universal impact on groups:

T–The **Type** of group must first be identified to accurately identify goals for processes and roles.

R–The **Role(s)** the leader(s) will play, and the roles that members hold or take on. This includes the specific strategies, group skills, and leadership skills required for the group being planned. This is essential for guiding the implementation process.

A–The **Audience** that the members make up, and others who might not be present but would be invested in the group's success.

T–The **Timeline** of the group, including the scheduling of the group, the projected schedule, and session details such as start and ending times.

E–The **Expected outcomes**, including the goals at the onset, those the audience hope for, and those that might emerge as the group unfolds.

This mnemonic is helpful to school counselors as a gauge that can be quickly calculated and analyzed to support a thoughtful understanding of the preparation, delivery, and evaluation of a group. Additionally, if a group is already in process, and the counselor notices that the group is stuck or less productive, this tool can be used to help the group leader explicitly understand where the group is in the process and identify solutions for meaningful change. Below we develop and expand the characteristics of this framework.

T–Type

In order to determine the role that the school counselor could take on when leading various groups, it is important to note the type of group. The different types of groups that school counselors may lead typically fit into three main categories, each described in more detail in the coming chapters. These are psychoeducational groups and counseling groups (Chapter 4) and task groups (Chapter 5). We intentionally increase in scope these categories and understand that within a school there are other types of groups that may not easily fit into these categories and/or the groups may in fact be a blend or hybrid. Specifically, these groups might include small counseling groups; 504 meetings that may include teachers and parents; Individualized Educational Plan (IEP) meetings that may include school administrators, parents, teachers, staff, and students; school-level committees that focus on supporting teachers and staff wellness (e.g., Sunshine) or promoting cohesion among school staff (e.g., social committee). Other types of groups include school leadership meetings, such as department meetings or intervention team meetings, and student leadership team meetings (e.g., student council).

THINK ABOUT IT ... LET'S REFLECT

- What types of groups have you been a part of in the schools?
- What groups are run on a daily/weekly/monthly basis that you are always a part of?
- Do you know what the goals/objectives of the group(s) are?
- Are the goals/objectives static, or do they evolve?
- Are the goals/objectives informed by policies, practices, another source, or a person?

R—The Role(s)

Having reflected on the different types of groups, now we can explore the different roles that leaders can take and that members will take on or currently hold. This truly could depend on given titles, but there are some "roles" that folks will play that are related less to their professional roles and more to their personality and the manner in which they function in groups. Examples of roles are group leader, facilitator, process observer, chair, cochair, cheerleader, and listener. Other roles could simply be counselor, administrator, parent, sibling, student, or friend. Just to be clear, the roles the school counselor will take must be intentional. The role the members may take on might not always be obvious, and sometimes may even be malicious. Leaders and members can be fair and balanced, helpful, and nice. Some may take on an activist role. Some leaders or members may take on the role of a token, pushover, slow and steady, guide, fiery, raging, smooth, builder, destroyer, confused, difficult, mysterious, enigmatic. As you can see, the roles are endless. However, gauging your leadership style and discovering the members' dispositions will be necessary.

THINK ABOUT IT ... LET'S REFLECT

- Have you led the groups, including the planning?
- Can you recall a time when you had to become a leader of the group in order to facilitate it?
- What role do you typically take when you're in a group?
- What might be contributing to the role you take?
- Are you consistently serving the same role?
- What role might you take as a group leader?
- If there are any differences between the group role or leader role, what might be reasons for this?

A—The Audience

Audience members include the people who are in attendance, such as teachers, students, staff, administrators, stakeholders, community members, business partners, PTA members, coaches, or mental health professionals. Audience members may also include those who might not be present but who may be invested in the group's success. For example, an academic success group for students who are identified as at-risk will include the direct audience of the students themselves; members of the indirect audience could include both the classroom teacher and the parents. The difference between the roles that the leaders and members take overlap with the audience; however, the audience is seen more as a collection of the individuals within or outside of the group who would be invested in the group's successes or failures.

THINK ABOUT IT ... LET'S REFLECT

- Who have you served most often in groups?
- How comfortable are you working with each audience identified?
- Do you receive professional development or continuous training to support your work with a variety of audiences and stakeholders served in the schools?
- What group(s) do you enjoy working with the most, and why?
- What group(s) do you find most challenging to work with in a group setting, and why?

T–The Timeline

The various timelines or scheduling considerations are dependent on deadlines that may be set before the onset of the group or after the group commences. The groups may meet for a predetermined number of hours or number of sessions or be based on the school calendar. The end goal is often determined at the beginning of the group. These timelines have an overall starting and ending timeframe, and the sessions also have a starting and ending time. The timeline is often adjusted based on the mandated tasks. If a group is set to meet once every grading marking period, then it will meet four times. If a group with parents is set to explore challenges helping their student transition from one grade level to the next, then the group may only meet for one session. That being said, different groups will determine how things unfold. Based on when each session will take place, the duration of each session, and the tasks that emerge, scheduling deadlines may need to be revisited over time. A number of factors need to be considered with regard to group timelines. For example, will the group occur repeatedly over the semesters; be based on certain seasons; or, if the work is longer than a school year, how are summer breaks handled and unforeseen circumstances (natural disasters, school closings) dealt with?

THINK ABOUT IT ... LET'S REFLECT

It is important to note that timelines may change. Snow days may interrupt the schedule. Pandemics may impact school schedules in dire ways. More common challenges include absences from the participants, changes in group leadership, and tasks getting completed faster or slower than anticipated.

- How do you prepare for the unexpected when taking the timelines into consideration?

E–The Expected Outcomes

Generally speaking, the different outcomes for most of the groups that are found in schools are academic, behavioral, or social in nature. They will include short-term as well as long-term goals.

Within the context of school counseling in particular, goals focus on achievement, attendance, or behavior. The goals are focused on individuals, segments of the school population, or the larger surrounding community. These goals align with student growth, event planning, PTA initiatives, and service-learning projects. For example, within a 504 meeting, the overall expected outcome might be the creation of a 504 plan; however, some suboutcomes might be to help the families understand their students' concerns more fully or having a new teacher feeling more comfortable providing valuable information to family participants.

THINK ABOUT IT ... LET'S REFLECT

- Is identification of expected outcomes a typical practice for meetings and groups in your school?
- As you consider this approach, how might this support your efficient work?
- As you consider the standing groups that you are a part of identified from earlier areas, do these existing groups have defined outcomes?
- Is the group meeting them?
- What is contributing to the success of meeting expected outcomes?
- What might be barriers, small or larger, to challenge reaching identified outcomes?

Application of the TRATE My Group Framework

Let's follow group leaders as they prepare to apply the TRATE My Group framework to meet a need in their school (see Figure 3.1). The group leaders might say to themselves, "Before beginning this group work (e.g., leadership team meeting, department meeting, 504 meeting), let's map out the group's TRATE to guide our planning and preparation for this group." Taking this action will help with content and process preparation as well as identify areas of additional information or resources needed before the group begins working to maximize efficiency and, in many schools, very limited resources. The application of technology will also need to be examined at every point in the TRATE process. Given busy schedules and video-conferencing fatigue, this preliminary step will positively impact the overall group dynamics.

Group leaders will ask themselves:

1. What *type* of group is this?
2. What *role* will I play in this specific group?
3. Who are all of the parties participating directly in this group as primary members of the *audience,* and who might be indirectly served or affected?
4. What *timeline* does this group have to complete the work required?
5. What are the *expected outcomes* that I am aware of at this point, as defined by me or another stakeholder?

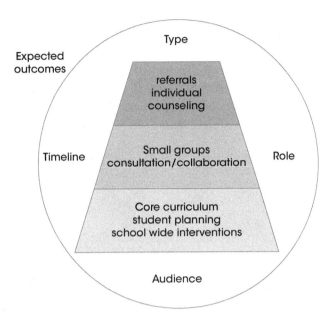

FIGURE 3.1. Integrated Applications of the TRATE My Group Framework

There will be some groups that will require the counselor to take an active leadership position from the start, such as sponsoring an afterschool club with middle school students conducting service-learning activities. In other examples, school counselors may be coleaders or serve more of a member role, such as during IEP meetings or 504 planning meetings with the students and their families, where a member from the special education department may be the recommended leader because of the topic area. Other examples that may offer variability in the predictable initial role for the counselor based on building level might include team meetings with teachers, staff and an academic department chair, serving on a district team for statewide or high-stakes testing, or contributing to the creation a schoolwide master schedule for the pending academic school year. We contend that there is an ongoing need for school counselors to be able to fulfill and support the many roles that are expected of them. Capitalizing on the power of group work is more imperative now than it ever has been due to the growing needs of students, families, and communities.

Pulling It All Together

School counselors can benefit from a deeper understanding and practical application of group work and its elements to directly benefit their efficient and productive contributions in PreK–12 schools. Continual reflective practices to engage and enhance group leadership and communication skills, along with mindful self-care and wellness strategies, are essential to the work of the group leader. To be the best helper one can be, the helpers must first take care of themselves! Awareness and recognition of cultural differences and similarities that affect environments and people will also aid the group leader in planning and preparation efforts as well as during facilitation of a group.

One way counselors can facilitate the intersectionality of these essential elements is to build on their knowledge base from their graduate training and apply the TRATE My Group framework to support the planning and delivery of any type of group they may be a part of or leading in their schools. As we consider the professional training and pulse of the field, this approach seeks to ground school counselors through a practical approach that maximizes evidenced-based practices while they are engaged in prevention and intervention services and supporting intentional, mindful, reflective practices.

DISCUSSION QUESTIONS

1. What influenced your choice to become a school counselor?

2. What do you recall from your personal experience with school counselors?

3. How did you learn about the role of a school counselor? In what way was it informed by an indirect experience, such as observing and/or supporting another person?

4. Did your school counselor run groups?

5. What were your experiences like if you participated in a group?

6. If a current school counselor, what is your involvement in leading groups?

7. What is the biggest influence on whether you facilitate groups or desire to lead groups?

REFERENCES

Bryan, J., Moore-Thomas, C., Day-Vines, N. L., Holcomb-McCoy, C. (2011). School counselors as social capital: The effects of high school college counseling on college application rates. *Journal of Counseling and Development, 89*(2), 190–199.

Tang, A., & Ng, K.-M. (2019). High school counselor contacts as predictors of college enrollment. *The Professional Counselor, 9*(4), 347–357. https://doi.org/10.15241/akt.9.4.347

Vannatta, R., & Steen, S. (2019). Pedagogical practices in CACREP-accredited group counseling courses: A content analysis. *Journal for Specialists in Group Work, 44*(2), 138–150.

Student-Level Groups

Counseling and Psychoeducation

I f you hear a clinical counselor or therapist say they plan to "run a group," regardless of the topic, they are likely referencing a counseling growth or psychotherapy group. These types of groups are common in supporting a myriad of topics and themes within the clinical space and can be adapted to a variety of clinical settings, including hospital, in-patient, outpatient, and residential settings. In a public PreK-12 school, however, psychotherapy groups are not expected to be offered due to the appropriateness of the topics for the school setting, logistical challenges, and sometimes the depth of training of the counselor in the school. The use of counseling growth groups is limited based on goodness of fit of the topic and the student members as well as the skill level of the school counselor for leading this type of group. As emphasized in Chapter 2, group counseling and group work is a continually practiced intentional skill set for practicing counselors, and it is not often a major focus of graduate training programs. The depth of subject matter knowledge and clinical experience required to lead counseling growth and psychotherapy groups may not have been attained by a practicing counselor in a school setting. These counselors are certainly capable to engage in this area of clinical training and development, because they possess the foundational knowledge and skills to do so, but the clinical practice may be lacking. As such, and compounded by the other logistical elements and ethical concerns for best practices, it is not common for psychotherapy groups to be offered in a public PreK-12 school, and specific topics will limit the types of counseling growth groups observed. In contrast, there are endless examples of task groups and psychoeducational groups to support and attend to student-level needs in PreK-12 schools.

Generally speaking, group counseling usually consists of at least 2 or more clients, not to exceed 12, who meet face to face or virtually using a multimedia platform, with 1 or 2 trained group clinical counselors/therapists. In the clinical group sessions, clients share what most concerns them, and the leaders work diligently to use their listening, reflecting, encouraging, and probing skills to foster cohesive spaces for members to engage in the session as they see fit. In some cases clients feel comfortable sharing thoughts and feelings about their lives. In other cases, clients are less comfortable disclosing what is in their hearts and minds due to any number of reasons, including fear, anxiety, self-doubt, or even hostility toward the group itself or the members. The group leaders help build a climate suitable for all members, and therefore their input is most valuable in determining how to use these sessions. The interactions occurring in the group, facilitated by the group leaders, give members an opportunity to increase understanding of self and others, try out new ways of being with others, and learn more effective ways to interact. As we consider this process and flow of the group process from a clinical lens and transition it to a public PreK-12 school setting, it is clear there is a lot of overlap and similarities among the members and the leaders.

When school counselors discuss "facilitating a small group" within the school setting, it will likely be either a counseling group or a psychoeducational group. Drilling down, we understand that there are important nuanced differences between the two. For instance, generally speaking, a psychoeducational group is highly structured, time limited, and focused on specific issues and behavioral goals identified prior to the session beginning (DeLucia-Waack, 2006). The interactions that occur within the group are leader centered, which means that they are intentionally driven by the group leader. This approach adapts easily to the developmental levels of children and adolescents, thus making it a "go to" choice for school counselors in the elementary, middle, or high school levels. Counseling growth groups will require a level of reflective thinking, communication skills, and interpersonal awareness or skills lending more aptly to serve middle or high school students based on basic maturation of normative human development.

Foundational Knowledge, Contextual Dimensions, and Practice

In schools we believe it is important to distinguish which group type is the best fit based on the goals of the group and the known members and the leader(s). Building on earlier chapters, we will take a more deliberate look at the efficacy of counseling and psychoeducational groups in schools informed by the emerging literature. After that, a deeper examination of the differences, similarities, benefits, and challenges of psychoeducational groups are discussed. Following this discussion, application of the TRATE My Group framework within the school setting to foster climates of inclusion and achievement is outlined. The objectives for this chapter are as follows:

1. Review the emerging academically focused and culturally appropriate group counseling research in school settings and its limitations.
2. Describe counseling groups in schools and identify the benefits and challenges of such groups.
3. Describe psychoeducational groups in schools and the benefits and challenges of such groups.
4. Briefly explain process observation and its ability to enhance group dynamics.
5. Apply psychoeducational groups to foster racially inclusive and supportive environments in schools.

Group Counseling Literature

School counselors have the requisite educational background and skill set to use group counseling interventions within school settings to meet an array of student developmental needs (American

School Counselor Association [ASCA], 2019). Although groups in school settings are promoted as being effective at addressing a variety of different issues for children and adolescents, the evidence in the literature still remains scarce (ASCA, 2019; Griffith et al., 2019). Specifically, the ASCA (2014) position statement on group counseling suggested that groups in school settings promote academic achievement and personal growth, yet more research is warranted concerning achievement outcomes.

Nonetheless, a number of studies have examined general areas of focus on children and adolescents in groups. Take for instance, a salient study by Hoag and Burlingame (1997). The reviewed 56 research articles and determined that group counseling has a significant and positive impact on children and adolescents. Other authors have found positive effects of group counseling for students on a broad range of measures (Prout & Prout, 1998). A leading researcher on groups argued within a conceptual article that group counseling serving students in school settings is effective and should be used more frequently as opportunities and needs continue to arise in the 21st century (Shechtman, 2002). Kulic and colleagues (2004) examined the efficacy of group treatments focused on primary prevention for children via a meta-analysis of group counseling studies over a 10-year span (1990–2000). Their meta-analysis revealed the following:

- The majority of these interventions occurred in a school setting.
- 75.6% used a treatment manual or specifically outlined their interventions.
- Half of the interventions lasted for 3 months or less.
- Half of the interventions were facilitated by a professional counselor with or without a coleader.

These results provide support that many groups in schools are facilitated with structured treatment manuals. Kulic et al. (2004) concluded that cognitive-behavioral interventions targeting specific issues such as depression in elementary schools (drawing from psychoeducational and counseling growth group types) were the most effective. It is important for school counselors to be aware of the research on groups for specific problems, because there is a great deal of variance in the efficacy of programs and in what can be done to make a program more effective. It is important for researchers and practitioners to work together to maximize the impact of group interventions in school settings and more practitioner focused research in schools is needed.

Academic-Focused Group Counseling Interventions

A study by Steen et al. (2021) examined 12 group counseling interventions that took place in school settings. The interventions selected required a specific focus on improving academic achievement–related outcomes (e.g., end-of-quarter grades, comprehensive exams, standardized tests, or grade point average). The authors discovered that those studies targeting comprehensive/comparative tests and GPA as the outcomes had the greatest impact (i.e., produced the highest effect sizes).

The review also included an examination of factors that may have had an impact on the effectiveness of these group interventions, such as use of protocol (i.e., highly structured intervention or not), the number of sessions for the group, and whether the racial demographics of the group leaders and members matched. Although there was some evidence that group interventions targeting achievement as an outcome could produce favorable results, the other factors were not clearly linked to these outcomes. Steen and colleagues (2021) noted the following implications emerging from their study:

- School counselors leading groups will need group training regardless of whether a structured manual is used. If a protocol is not used, group training will be necessary to ensure treatment fidelity.
- Research that focuses on groups in school settings is very much still needed in order to better inform policy makers, school administrators, school counselors, and other staff about the duration of an intervention in order to make a difference in students' academic performance.
- In some cases when the group leaders and students were matched on racial demographics, it positively impacted the effectiveness of group interventions on student academic achievement. However, more nuanced investigation could account for the impact of these different demographic variables in order to determine the best combination of group leader and student characteristics.
- Finally, it is recommended to discover more ways to measure academic outcomes or alter the groups' content/interventions to more directly meet the requirements of the academic measures. Paying attention only to standardized testing and GPA might not always be feasible as an outcome for group interventions in school settings.

Table 4.1 summarizes research on specific efforts by researchers to include culturally diverse group interventions in school settings (S. Steen, personal communication, May 4, 2020). The main purpose in presenting this sample of studies is to explore the topics, to summarize their content, and to examine the relationship between academic achievement and broad aspects of culture when presented for children and adolescents in school settings.

TABLE 4.1   Examples of Culturally Inclusive Group Counseling Interventions in School Settings

Author	Article Title	Summary	Notes
Muller and Hartman (1998)	Group counseling for sexual minority youth	This article reviews the issues facing sexual minority youth by presenting a model of counseling in schools. This LGBTQ youth counseling group was conducted in a high school in Maryland.	No findings were presented.
Muller (2000)	A 12-session, European American–led counseling group for African American females	New programs arise as schools become more aware of and sensitive to the need to reach out to minority students. The following group was designed for and implemented in a suburban high school in Baltimore, Maryland.	African American students comprised about 20% of the school population. It was apparent that young African American women dealt with multiple levels of discrimination and faced issues of sexism.

(Continued)

TABLE 4.1 (Continued)

Author	Article Title	Summary	Notes
Muller (2002)	Group counseling for African American males: When all you have are European American counselors	This article presents information on the design, implementation, and assessment of a 12-week school counseling group for high school African American males led by European American female counselors.	No findings were presented.
Campbell and Brigman (2005)	Closing the achievement gap: A structured approach to group counseling	This study evaluated the impact of a group counseling intervention on student academic and social performance. Twenty-five school counselors were trained to use a structured approach to small group counseling with students scoring in the mid to low range in math and reading. The group intervention focused on improving student achievement and student success skills, which included academic, social, and self-management skills.	Results indicated gains in reading and math achievement scores and in teacher-rated behavior related to student success skills with elementary and middle school students.
Steen and Kaffenberger (2007)	Integrating academic interventions into small group counseling in elementary school	This article is a summary and evaluation of a small group counseling program that targets academic issues while addressing personal/social issues with elementary-aged children.	Results suggested that integrating academic interventions and group counseling improved students' behavior related to school achievement. Presented implications for school counselors and application of the ASCA National Model.
Bruce, Getch, and Ziomek-Daigle (2009)	Closing the gap: A group counseling approach to improve test performance of African American students	This article evaluated the impact of a group counseling intervention on African American students' achievement rates during the spring administration of high-stakes testing at a rural high school in Georgia.	Eighty percent of eligible students who participated in the intervention received passing scores on the four sections of the Georgia High School Graduation Tests, and all participating students received passing scores on the English Language Arts and Math sections.

(Continued)

TABLE 4.1   **(Continued)**

Author	Article Title	Summary	Notes
Kayler and Sherman (2009)	At-risk ninth-grade students: A psycho-educational group approach to increase study skills and grade point averages	The purpose of this article is to describe a large-scale psychoeducational study skills group for ninth-grade students whose academic performance is in the bottom 50% of their class. The ASCA National Model was used as a framework for development, delivery, and evaluation.	The authors found that a small-group counseling intervention strengthened studying behaviors as measured by pretest–posttest design. Additional results included the need to promote school counselor visibility and to increase and improve school counselor relationships with students, parents, and other stakeholders.
Steen (2009)	Group counseling for African American elementary students: An exploratory study	This article describes a group counseling intervention promoting academic achievement and ethnic identity development for 20 fifth-grade African American elementary students.	The Multigroup Ethnic Identity Measure (MEIM) scores of students participating in the treatment group improved significantly over those in the control group.
Amatea, Thompson, Rankin-Clemons, and Ettinger (2010)	Becoming partners: A school-based group intervention for families of young children who are disruptive	A multiple-family discussion group program was implemented and evaluated by school counselors working with families of young children referred by their teachers for aggression and attention problems. The logic guiding construction of the program and the program's unique aspects are described.	Outcome data revealed that the program was effective in reducing the children's hyperactive, defiant, and aggressive behavior and improving the parents' management skills.
Malott, Paone, Humphreys, and Martinez (2010)	Use of group counseling to address ethnic identity development: Application with adolescents of Mexican descent	This article provides qualitative outcomes from a group counseling intervention whose goal was to facilitate the ethnic identity development of Mexican-origin youth.	Outcomes revealed that participants perceived group participation as meaningful. Themes that emerged from the data included the importance of the relationship to engender change, growth in several aspects of ethnic identity (knowledge of culture, traits, and ethnic pride), and increased relational skills.

(Continued)

TABLE 4.1   **(Continued)**

Author	Article Title	Summary	Notes
Davis, Davis, and Mobley (2013)	School counselor's role in addressing the advanced placement equity and excellence gap for African American students	This study describes the collaboration among a school counselor, a school counselor intern, an Advanced Placement Psychology teacher, and a counselor educator to improve African American access to Advanced Placement (AP) coursework and increase success on the AP Psychology national examination.	The team initiated a process that recruited African American students into AP Psychology and supported them through group and individual counseling and supported them through group and individual counseling to create an achievement-minded cohort that emphasized peer relationships and academic success.
Rose and Steen (2014)	The Achieving Success Everyday group counseling model: Fostering resiliency in middle school students	The authors aimed to discover what impact this group counseling intervention, which focused on resiliency characteristics, would have on students' academic and personal-social success. To evaluate this, the authors used both qualitative and quantitative data.	The results showed that some students achieved an increase in their GPA and personal-social functioning following the intervention.
Steen, Liu, Shi, Rose, and Merino (2018)	Promoting school adjustment for English-language learners through group work	The goal of this study was to conduct a school-based group counseling intervention with a high-risk population of students recently immigrated to the United States to determine whether attitudes about learning, self-esteem, school adjustment, and academic performance could be improved.	Results showed that students in the treatment group received significantly higher scores on school adjustment after controlling for preintervention scores. Students' GPAs also increased following the intervention. Through reflections in journals, students were able to express some of their personal and private thoughts and feelings.

Limitations

Although emerging research can be gleaned from the literature, the body of work needs to grow. Psychoeducational groups, as mentioned earlier, are very common in schools and agencies, but the published articles presented do not typically fit into this category when exploring the research. The common terminology used between counseling groups and psychoeducational groups also adds to the confusion. For instance, groups in schools, whether counseling or psychoeducational, promote personal and interpersonal growth and development and aim to address or prevent future difficulties.

As discussed in Chapter 2, the differences between the two may be subtle, and without training, might appear the same. In either case, these groups can be adapted and modified to meet the developmental level of the members that comprise the group, making these group types adaptable to working with children and adolescents of all ages. One specific difference could be that counseling groups typically use more liberty to ebb and flow on the degree of structure used in the group or session to meet counseling depth and therapeutic factors emerging from the experience. Nonetheless, below we aim to spell out the differences between a counseling group and a psychoeducational group, as well as provide some examples of benefits and challenges, respectively.

Counseling Groups: Benefits and Challenges

A counseling group is designed to help students deal with interpersonal issues and promote changes in behavior related to these problems. As a result, a counseling group is often used as an intervention, with one goal being an overt change in the problematic or concerning behaviors initially identified. The group topic or theme is problem oriented, inviting and allowing the leader to channel the interactions that occur within the group to help each of the members identify their own understanding, meaning, and resolutions to the challenges experienced within and outside of the group. Counseling groups such as this are often considered "closed." This means that the student members of the group will not vary from session to session, and even though some students may be tardy or absent at times, the membership remains the same. This stability in membership facilitates trust building and group cohesion. The consistency of the students allows each member to potentially consider and ultimately invest in the group (e.g., other students, leaders) directly. Each member will work and grow in their own unique ways to meet their individual goals, and they will support and encourage their members to do the same even though it is always not clear which critical incidents (e.g., salient interactions that occur within the group) lead to this deeper personal growth and insight.

The goals of counseling groups include helping the members give and receive support, helping members gain a deeper understanding of presenting problems, and helping members think through possible ways to combat these difficulties. Counseling groups foster engagement between members and stimulate interactions with others to practice social skills in a confidential and safe environment. These interactions often lead to opportunities for the students to give and receive feedback on the manner in which they are seen by one another and among each other.

Counseling groups help the participants participate collectively in solving problems, sharing emotional experiences, and mitigating feelings of isolation. Although these groups can be helpful in exploring specific presenting problems, there is a focus on content (topic up for discussion) and a focus on process (reactions and reflections on the underlying thoughts and feelings on what's being discussed). There is no set amount of content or process that is needed; however, there is indeed a balance between content and process, distinguishing this type of group from a psychoeducational group, which often fails to include an examination of the process.

Counseling groups in various forms are quite common in school settings. However, there are some limitations to these in their truest form. For instance, counseling groups focus on member interactions and require that a solid foundation of cohesion emerges. In school settings this could occur quickly if the students already know each other, or it could be more difficult simply because the students already know each other due to the conflict that has already existed outside of the group. Additionally, once this cohesion is present, it will take time for members to feel comfortable enough to share what is on their minds and in their hearts. Oftentimes, these groups in school settings only occur over about 6 to 12 sessions (Erford, 2018) and for approximately 30 minutes. The major challenge with these time limitations is that more structure will be needed to get to the presenting problems and then to have students engage in deeper reflections. Facilitating an environment that fosters opportunities to share more deeply requires time. This could mean having more sessions or longer sessions, but there are time constraints in school settings (Steen et al., 2021). Oftentimes, school counselors hear exclamations from students once the group is coming to an end that they would like it to continue. This is not an unusual sentiment in most groups, but the challenge in a school is that there is not an endless amount of time, and there are many other competing factors.

Other limitations include logistics, such as finding a confidential space, and timing being limited to the academic school building schedule. For example, students who may be appropriate members of the same group may have different academic schedules that do not align; the primary goal of the student in the traditional PreK-12 school building is for academic growth and development—not for therapeutic groups. In some cases a student might benefit from a counseling group, but because this student also needs other forms of remediation and is pulled out of class, they may not have the chance to also be pulled out for the group. Counseling groups are powerful, and despite these limitations they can be used to work at helping students achieve goals identified by their teachers, parents/guardians, their peers, and themselves.

THINK ABOUT IT ... LET'S REFLECT

Imagine that your school administration wants you to run a group for every new student who registers for your school after the school year begins. Consider the following questions to explore the complexities required for purposeful group planning and preparation to meet this seemingly simple request.

- Where do you begin?
- What type of group will you develop?
- What is the topic or primary focus of the group?
- Is the topic versatile to meet the various developmental levels of the students initially targeted for the group?
- How many sessions will the students need to attend?
- When will the group take place?
- Where will the sessions occur?
- How will the information be differentiated based on the members' academic needs?
- Will this be run as an open or closed group?
- What will you do for those students who are still learning English?
- How will you ensure that race and culture are infused in the interventions?
- Will these sessions be led with another leader, and if so, with whom?
- What are other questions that are important as you consider your school and primary populations served?

Psychoeducational Groups: Benefits and Challenges

Psychoeducational groups serve students in small groups or entire classrooms of students. The highly structured environment lessens anxiety for the members and leaders because the expectations are clear. Psychoeducational groups use clear goals and objectives. These goals are stated explicitly at the beginning, are revisited periodically during a session or the group, and are reassessed at the end to ensure optimal outcomes. Psychoeducational groups have a distinct component that includes teaching the members specific learning objectives; however, learning also occurs naturally among the members as spontaneous interactions emerge. Psychoeducational groups are time limited; this means that the topics, goals, and objectives are clearly identified at the beginning and the number of sessions needed to accomplish these specific goals is determined prior to the group's commencement. The highly structured environment is facilitated in a manner such that it could be replicated, even though it is impossible for any group to unfold exactly as the way it is intended because there are so many unknowns that happen when a group of people are interacting. There is a mixture of content and brief opportunities to reflect on what was learned and how this could apply to one's life.

Psychoeducational groups in a school setting may have two distinct yet interrelated definitions. First, groups with a small number of students might be referred to as a counseling group, but actually it may be a psychoeducational group. Second, school counselors teach counseling curricula to a large number of students (i.e., entire classrooms full of students) as part of their work that are known as classroom guidance lessons, but are technically psychoeducational groups facilitated within the classroom.

Psychoeducational groups are much more structured than counseling groups. As we consider applications in a school setting and working with children and adolescents, the structure inherent in psychoeducational groups aligns best with their developmental level. Abstract thinking and a deeper level of self-awareness is often observed later in adolescence and emerging adulthood, according to normative brain, cognitive, emotional, and moral development. Psychoeducational groups are focused on specific topics, and the information is delivered directly to the students. Psychoeducational groups are designed in order to provide a venue to impart information to the students, to have members share similarities and differences associated with the topic for discussion, to teach members problem-solving strategies, and to identify individuals and systems of support within the group and outside of the meetings. There is an emphasis on the topic in order to help the students gain knowledge and skills. There also may be opportunities for reflecting on any insight gained, but the expectation is that the major focus is on the content and minimally on the process.

Some psychoeducational groups are framed to help educate members, some are framed to focus on specific skill acquisition, and some are framed on gaining a deeper understanding of oneself, which is in fact similar to a counseling group. The major difference is that there is less focus on self-disclosing and more focus on giving and receiving feedback about how interactions among the students are interpreted and impacting those involved.

Psychoeducational groups aim to teach students about a wide range of issues. For example, anger management is a common topic that students may learn about. Of course, anger management may have a negative connotation, so a psychoeducational group that wants to include skills that would be applicable to gaining emotional regulation might be simply termed *social skills, friendship group, communication skills*, and so forth. Other broad topics include body weight issues, managing stress, grief and loss, healthy eating, substance use pressures, social media usage, career choices, college exploration, and celebrating racial and ethnic diversity.

Classroom Guidance

The focus here is on small psychoeducational groups, but this information is applicable also to classroom guidance. Embedded within the ASCA National Model (2019) is a recommended delivery mode referred to as *school counseling core curriculums*. This effort will push into a classroom setting to deliver a lesson or provide guidance on a topic or theme. It may be delivered in collaboration with the classroom teacher or other counselors, or it may be delivered with only one counselor. It may take the entire class period for one session or involve repeated sessions over several weeks. Depending on the topic, sometimes there are interconnected assignments, with the classroom being used to reach the students. For example, counselors who may use a classroom guidance approach to deliver information to the junior class regarding financial aid and postsecondary planning may find it helpful to work with the English department. This is a required course for 11th graders, assisting the counselor to reach all students in the general curriculum. Given the topic area on future plans after high school, the counselor may collaborate with the English department and faculty such that following the counselors presentation the students have a classroom assignment that will help them practice the skills and knowledge gleaned in English while also reflecting and considering the new information shared by the counselor.

As we consider psychoeducational groups, it is important to first recognize that the topics discussed can be linked to important areas of focus within the general curriculum. Second, the academic or career focus could be linked within service-learning opportunities or other real-world applications. Third, it is feasible for a psychoeducational group to be only one session long. The specific stated goals and objectives might be written in a manner that requires only one session.

While taking into consideration some of the benefits of facilitating psychoeducational groups in schools, there are a few challenges. For instance, confidentiality is more difficult to maintain. The topics up for discussion in many cases are generic enough that the members will discuss this information with others to build on what they learned. These conversations increase the chances that what was shared in the group does not stay there. Another concern is that while these groups can be brief and even just one session, it is difficult to sustain any learning or growth that may have occurred. There may also be logistics unique to a school setting, topics or themes best suited for psychoeducational group approaches, and time barriers. Common logistical limitations include the academic schedule of the students identified as benefiting from being members in the same group. Because the primary purpose for the students to be in the school building is for academic growth, there can be challenges to finding flexible time in their academic schedules that will permit a full academic period available to be a part of group. This can also be a challenge when most schools build schedules follow a 6- or 7-day rotation schedule or waterfall-style schedule; thus, a "Monday" is not necessarily going to be the exact same schedule every calendar Monday as it might be in the working world. Lastly, psychoeducational groups spend more time delivering information and less time exploring one's feelings and reactions to the concepts being presented, and members may desire more time to think, feel, and act on what they are learning. More specifically, some students may believe that this type of group is boring because it resembles an all-too-familiar classroom environment with the set structure and less flexible game plan.

As mentioned earlier, there are several topics that can fit within a psychoeducational group approach; however, in a school setting, various topics may be limiting or taboo in some communities. For example, learning about gender-nonconforming individuals might be less appropriate in school systems that are hesitant to acknowledge the realities for some members for fear of backlash from parents worried that exposure to this topic implies encouraging young people to align with these experiences.

Another nuanced challenge is the fact that being able to engage and reach the depth needed in the group experience and group process takes time. This is specifically the time spent building upon each session, but also time during each session to go through the phases of that one group session. In a school setting, students are often coming to the group from various classes and locations in the building, which may include having to first check in with a classroom teacher. On the back end, the counselor must be mindful of the time, ensuring that sufficient time remains before the bell rings and the student needs to return to their "usual flow" as a student in the school attentive and engaged in all remaining classes for the day. Thus, counselors must be cautious when navigating schedules, specific themes, or time considerations in these important groups.

Despite the limitations noted above, psychoeducational groups are still a viable way to go about meeting the needs of youngsters. Psychoeducational groups can infuse board games, role-play, toys, and other fun props for students to actively participate in the learning. Common psychoeducational groups in schools can include the same topics as counseling groups but differ in that the entire curriculum can be determined ahead of time. The topics can include anything that is relevant to the students themselves or their academic and career goals. Once a topic is identified clear definitions are needed, goals and objectives must be created and a few takeaways identified that will be important to ensure enough structure is provided to the participants.

Process Observation

Process is one of the unique treasurers of group counseling and group work overall. As explained in Chapter 2, *group process* often explains the "how" in the counseling experience seeking to better understand inter- and intrapersonal dynamics as a part of the group. It is often one of the most advanced skills and techniques to master, and one of the most complex constructs to understand. The counselor who is able to employ process observation is able to receive information from multiple perspectives, simultaneously attending to the group as a whole, each individual member, and how they are experiencing the group as the group leader. This multitasking is done while the actual group is occurring. In training for individual practice, counselors learn the skill of a "dual dialogue" whereby they are able to truly listen to the individual client and engage them with questions, comments, etc., all while also having an internal dialogue in their mind considering, assessing, dismissing, and saving thoughts and information that are relevant to helping the client work toward their identified treatment goals. In group counseling, process observation is similar, and magnified both in terms of increasing perspectives of information input as well as the number of individuals who are attended to.

Leaders to the field of group counseling and therapy, Yalom and Leszcz (2020), states it best:

> Before therapists can help clients understand the process, they must themselves learn to recognize it: in other words, they must be able to reflect in the midst of the group inter-action and wonder, "why is *this* unfolding in this group in this particular way and at this particular time?" The experienced therapist does this naturally and effortlessly, observing the group proceedings from several different perspectives, including the specific individual interactions and the developmental issues in the group. (p. 165)

A counselor or group leader's ability to process and provide process observations during the group experience contributes to a unique richness that each member and the group as a whole can benefit from. It enhances the opportunities for reflection, awareness, and meaningful interpretation of the therapeutic factors for each member and the leader as they consider their role and the group as a whole.

Although the application and benefit of engaging in process observation is clear when considering its role as a part of counseling groups and a therapeutic setting, we invite school counselors to consider adapting the use of process observation as an intentional technique to assist them in their psychoeducational and task group work most commonly observed on a daily basis in a school setting. We also focus on psychoeducational and task groups specifically, because these often are limited in the depth and richness that they are able to offer. Application of our TRATE My Group framework invites the expansion of consideration to prepare and facilitate these types of groups, regardless of the duration or what the topic of focus may be. The counselor will be able to add depth and meaning to the work, while also engaging in efficient and best practice, and invite others in the group to do the same through direct action and role modeling.

Culturally Relevant and Ethically Sound Application of the TRATE My Group Framework

As shared in Chapter 3, the TRATE My Group framework is adaptable for planning and imple-mentation based on what type of group the counselor intends to facilitate. This works well for psychoeducational sessions that are focused a bit more on content, with some sprinkles of process and intentionality at making them adaptable to small group settings or classrooms. It can help to engage students or members of the psychoeducational group in an interactive way as they are receiving the information shared, yielding potentially greater outcomes.

This framework can be helpful to guide counselors in the planning stage for school-based inter-ventions when they are leading groups in the school. The TRATE my group framework is also helpful to plan, deliver, and evaluate noncounseling-related groups and activities, such as PTA, parent, or staff meetings. Regardless of whether the counselor notices that the group is stuck or less productive, this tool can be used to help the group leaders explicitly understand where they are in the process and identify solutions for meaningful change.

TRATE My Group Framework

T – The **Type** of group is identified to most accurately identify goals and processes.

R –The **Role(s)** the leader(s) will play, and the roles that members hold or take on, are identified.

A – The **Audience** that the members make up, and others who might not be present but would be invested in the group's success, are identified.

T – The **Timeline** of the group, including the scheduling of the group, the projected schedule, and session details such as start and ending times, is determined.

E – The **Expected outcomes**, including the goals at the onset, those the audience hope for, and those that might emerge as the group unfolds, are identified.

Consider the following example inspired by real situations counselors encounter in PreK-12 schools. The TRATE My Group framework is applied as a way to assist this counselor to balance meeting the needs of the school community and the parents and families through a counseling growth group delivery mode.

Example Situation

The other day, a school district administrator shared the following with parents and families of students attending this school in this particular school district:

> *Dear Bullfrog High School Families,*
>
> *Our Public School District has been made aware that a Bullfrog High School student recently posted insensitive and racist comments on social media regarding several racial and ethnic groups in the Our Community. Racism in any form is not acceptable in Our Community and we denounce the behavior of this student. Their comments do not reflect the values of our community. This matter is being investigated by the Bullfrog High School administration, and it will be addressed according to Our Community policy. Additionally, due to the nature of this post the Sheriff's Office has been notified, and we are working with them on this matter."*

While much of the focus in this chapter has been on psychoeducational groups, we would like to apply the TRATE My Group framework in this example as a counseling group. A counseling group intervention or a psychoeducational intervention could be used to address this problem within this particular high school. The use of a counseling group seems reasonable if the focus is on building agency and providing support for the victims of these racist social media posts. If the perpetrator were the focus of the intervention, then a psychoeducational group would be appropriate.

The number of increasingly bold, insensitive, violent, cruel, and racially aggressive media posts from both children and adults seems to be increasing. Some might argue that the children are posting information they are hearing within the home (i.e., *parroting*, or repeating what they are hearing from their families and communities without actually understanding the depth of what they are saying). If this is the case, then mimicking what they are hearing from their adult family members might be more difficult to compete with, because parents rightfully hold major influence over their children, even when the values espoused contradict the expectations of the school. Other explanations could be that students are reading material posted on social media that is used to inform them of such cruelty that they either perpetuate themselves based on what they have read or confirms what they have heard outside of schools on the playground, playing field, or other social gathering or clubs. Illustrated is a group intervention that could be used to work with the victims applying the TRATE My Group framework.

T – The **Type** of group will be a counseling group. The purpose of the group will be to offer a space to mitigate the negative impact experienced by those who have been targeted by the inappropriate messages on social media regarding Bullfrog High School. While the school and school district are assessing these messages, and plan to eventually take some form of action and, if warranted, get law enforcement involved, this counseling group can be employed to provide social and emotional support to the students involved or impacted. In this case, the group could serve the victim, perpetrator, or both.

R – The **Role(s)** the leader(s) will play, and the roles that members hold or take on, must include risk taking in general. Specifically, the role the leaders will play will include one of facilitator and encourager. The leaders will need to be open to modeling strategies they would consider using if this would have happened to them, self-disclosing experiences that they have encountered, if relevant. Honesty will be an important component in this type of group whether or not the leaders have ever been the target of racism. The leaders can draw upon their experiences with oppression or feelings of inferiority, but it will be crucial that the examples disclosed are to generate brave spaces for the members to share their experiences. If the leaders are unable to relate or they have less personal experience with this particular form of racism and discrimination, their willingness to share this truth can offer important opportunities for the members to reflect upon. In other words, it is more important for the leader to be honest than it is for them to be an expert, well-versed on the topic, or avoidant. The role the students can take or hold could present in the following manner. Due to the nature of the topic, students may choose to remain quiet. Students may be angry. Some will be confused, and many may be sad. The students may be experiencing these feelings of discrimination for the first time; others may hold intersecting identities that increase the likelihood they have experienced forms of racism and discrimination before. It is important to note that this applies to the group leader as well.

A – The **Audience**, first and foremost, is the students themselves who have been directly impacted by these atrocities. Other ancillary audience members include stakeholders who might not be present but who would be invested in the group's success, such as the families, community members, and school faculty and staff. The fact that social media is the vehicle used to spread this racial tension and derogatory messaging inherently impacts the school and community.

T – The **Timeline** depends on the scheduling of the group, the projected schedule, and session details such as start and ending times. In this case, time will be needed to recruit and screen members to determine if they are victims, perpetrators, or bystanders and witnesses. The schedule for this type of group could be weekly meetings in person or virtually. The sessions should not be shorter than 40 minutes, and ideally would be 50 minutes to provide ample time to process the information. The number of sessions is constrained by the school calendar, but group counseling interventions are more effective if they aim for at least 20 sessions but no fewer than 12 (Steen et al., in press).

E - The **Expected outcomes** or goals for this group intervention are to provide a brave space for students who have been impacted by the racist remarks on social media. The objective of this group is to facilitate open and honest discussions about the participants' thoughts, feelings, and behaviors. Other objectives include providing a safe space to receive feedback about one's strengths to overcome these negative actions and to discuss strategies members can use to combat these posts in productive ways. In addition to exploring one's strengths to mitigate this discrimination, members can work together to develop a plan of action to use when it happens again. The goals at the onset are general enough for the group leader to modify them as things unfold. The major goal of this group would be to support students who have received racist comments via social media posts.

Pulling It All Together

Groups are an efficient and effective delivery mode to address complex topics with diverse groups of students. The two primary types of groups that adapt best to the public school setting to help students are counseling and psychoeducational groups. The Association for Specialists in Group Work provides guidelines for counselors to lead groups based on best practices, training standards, and multicultural and social justice principles. Generally speaking, these guidelines provide language to plan, deliver, and evaluate groups while also emphasizing the necessity to attend to race, ethnicity, culture, and the complex interplay among the group leader and members. School counselors must balance the needs of students and their families and teachers' expectations related to educational goals.

Psychoeducational groups can be the best option most of the time in the public school setting to meet the needs of a diverse student population. These groups provide a powerful venue to teach knowledge and skills while reflecting in small ways any insight gained about themselves or their peers.

DISCUSSION QUESTIONS

1. What developmental considerations need to be explored when deciding whether to use psychoeducational groups versus counseling groups?

2. Which group most appropriately fits into response to intervention or multi-tiered systems of support, psychoeducational or counseling groups?

3. Students often complain that psychoeducational groups mirror their classroom experience. How do you go about ensuring that their group experience is unique?

4. What guidance should you use to determine how much process to include in psychoeducational groups?

5. As you think about process observation skills, where have you used these skills, unbeknownst to you, and where do you plan to use these skills in the future?

REFERENCES

Amatea, E. S., Thompson, I. A., Rankin-Clemons, L., & Ettinger, M. L. (2010). Becoming partners: A school-based group intervention for families of young children who are disruptive. *Journal of School Counseling, 8*, 1–31.

American School Counselor Association. (2014). *The school counselor and group counseling.*

American School Counselor Association. (2019). *The ASCA national model: A framework for school counseling programs* (4th ed.).

Bruce, A. M., Getch, Y. Q., & Ziomek-Daigle, J. (2009). Closing the gap: A group counseling approach to improve test performance of African-American students. *Professional School Counseling, 12*, 450–457. https://doi.org/10.1177/2156759X0901200603

Campbell, C. A., & Brigman, G. (2005). Closing the achievement gap: A structured approach to group counseling. *Journal for Specialists in Group Work, 30*(1), 67–82.

Davis, P., Davis, M. P., & Mobley, J. A. (2013). The school counselor's role in addressing the advanced placement equity and excellence gap for African American students. *Professional School Counseling, 17*(1), 32–39.

DeLucia-Waack, J. L. (2006). *Leading psychoeducational groups for children and adolescents.* SAGE.

Erford, B. T. (Ed.). (2018). *Group work: Processes and applications.* Routledge.

Griffith, C., Mariani, M., McMahon, H. G., Zyromski, B., & Greenspan, S. B. (2019). School counseling intervention research: A 10-year content analysis of ASCA- and ACA-affiliated journals. *Professional School Counseling, 23*, 1–12. https://doi.org/10.1177/2156759X19878700

Hoag, M. J., & Burlingame, G. M. (1997). Evaluating the effectiveness of child and adolescent group treatment: A meta-analytic review. *Journal of Clinical Child Psychology, 26*, 234–246. https://doi.org/10.1207/s15374424jccp2603

Kayler, H., & Sherman, J. (2009). At-risk ninth-grade students: A psychoeducational group approach to increase study skills and grade point averages. *Professional School Counseling, 12*, 434–439. https://doi.org:10.5330/PSC.n.2010-12.434

Kulic, K. R., Horne, A. M., & Dagley, J. C. (2004). A comprehensive review of prevention groups for children and adolescents. *Group Dynamics: Theory, Research, and Practice, 8*(2), 139.

Malott, K. M., Paone, T. R., Humphreys, K., & Martinez, T. (2010). Use of group counseling to address ethnic identity development: Application with adolescents of Mexican descent. *Professional School Counseling, 13*(5), https://doi.org/10.1177/2156759X1001300502

Muller, L., E. (2000). A 12-session European American led group counseling intervention for African American females. *Professional School Counseling, 3*, 264–270.

Muller, L. E. (2002). Group counseling for African American males: When all you have are European American counselors. *Journal for Specialists in Group Work, 27*(3), 299–313.

Muller, L. E., & Hartman, J. (1998). Group counseling for sexual minority youth. *Professional School Counseling, 1*(3), 38–41.

Prout, S. M., & Prout, H. T. (1998). A meta-analysis of school-based studies of counseling and psychotherapy: An update. *Journal of School Psychology, 36*, 121–136. https://doi.org/10.1016/S0022-4405(98)00007-7

Rose, J., & Steen, S. (2014). The Achieving Success Everyday group counseling model: Fostering resiliency in middle school students. *Professional School Counseling, 18*, 28–37. https://doi.org/10.1177/2156759X0001800116

Shechtman, Z. (2002). Child group psychotherapy in the school at the threshold of a new millennium. *Journal of Counseling and Development, 80*, 293–299. https://doi.org/10.1002/j.1556-6678.2002.tb00194.x

Steen, S. (2009). Group counseling for African American elementary students: An exploratory study. *Journal for Specialists in Group Work, 34*(2), 101–117.

Steen, S., & Kaffenberger, C.J. (2007). Integrating academic interventions into group counseling with elementary students. *Professional School Counseling, 10*, 516–519.

Steen, S., Liu, X., Rose, J., & Merino, G. (2018). Promoting school adjustment for English-as-Second-Language students in group work: Implications for school counseling practice-based research. *Professional School Counseling, 21*, 1–10.

Steen, S., Shi, Q., & Melfie, J. (2021). School-based group counseling interventions and academic achievement: A comparative review of studies. *Journal of School-Based Counseling Policy and Evaluation, 3*(1), 1-13.

Yalom, I. D., & Leszcz, M. (2020). *The theory and practice of group psychotherapy.* Basic Books.

Building-Level Groups

Counselors Planning and Leading Task Groups

Commonly, when we think of group work in school settings we picture intervention groups directly serving students. Stretching our perspectives slightly, we can clearly see how task groups are used on a daily basis by several adult stakeholders at the building level as well as in community partnerships serving the schools. Although this may be more common in other fields such as project management or business, it is unlikely to find active discussions occurring about task groups in a school setting as a strategic conversation to inform productivity, goals, and outcomes. Why is that given that task groups are used so often in the schools? One possibility is the hyperfocus on intervention services and meeting of academic achievement goals, such that the collective "we" may have overlooked opportunities to discuss and outline the importance of other strategies for effective communication. However, if we can increase efficiency around the use and evaluation of task groups in schools, it stands to reason that the outcome will positively affect intervention services and academic achievement goals. There are very few resources to guide school counselors and building leaders about how to even begin, much less be effective. Using the TRATE My Group framework is one step to expanding the perspective of the group to inform planning and preparation. We introduce another framework that may further aid this effort called SMART goals that first contributed to the business and project management fields and has evolved within education to be a strategic tool for aiding children and adults. Although every case and scenario may have unique features that inhibit a true formula approach as to the "how" of implementation, we focus on strengthening a new perspective of how task groups are used in the schools coupled with the group leadership skills of the counselor as the building blocks for success.

School counselors are prepared during graduate school to facilitate evidence-based practices. They are charged to use data to drive accountable practices that are ethical and equity based in order to address the prevention and intervention needs throughout the school and surrounding community. Essential to this success is active collaboration with school administration, school staff, and other stakeholders identified within the school. A broad and intentional programmatic focus that includes a wide variety of perspectives and roles within the school to support common goals will enhance the opportunities for favorable outcomes (Schumacher & Ache, 2014). As you read this chapter and reflect on your practical experiences running groups in school settings, and task groups in particular for adults and students within a school, be sure to consider how professional educators are attempting to prepare you for what the realities are within our nation's schools.

Foundational Knowledge, Contextual Dimensions, and Practice

This chapter will offer examples to clarify how the efficiency and effectiveness of task groups can be enhanced with the intentional application and integration of key group work elements. We infuse understanding of human development and functioning, using group-based educational, developmental, and systemic strategies to foster best practice and effectiveness. The objectives for this chapter are as follows:

1. Identify new perspectives for how task groups may be a cornerstone to effective and efficient work in a school setting considering common benefits and challenges.
2. Discuss the role of task groups as an effective approach to engage and collaborate with children and adolescents.
3. Discuss the role of task groups as an effective approach to engage and collaborate with adults within and external to the school building.

A common group type utilized across the PreK-12 school levels is the *task group*. As the name implies, these types of groups have a charge, or a "task," to focus the work of the individuals that make up the group. Although there may be significant variety among topics, task groups are one essential way organizations with multiple members accomplish their work. If you consider your schedule recently, how many task groups have you been a member of that perhaps you may not have referred to as such?

Task Groups in School Settings

It is critical to understand the context as well as the primary audience being served when considering how to plan and facilitate a task group for a successful outcome. How we plan and facilitate a group composed of school staff, school administration, or variations of a school leadership team meeting will look drastically different than how we may structure a postsecondary planning and exploration group composed of middle school or high school students. Given the adaptability and flexibility demands of a school counselor, task groups are an essential tool that can be useful to help meet the needs of the school community.

Task groups provide opportunities for community collaboration, strengthening critical partnerships and relationships within the school building and larger school community. Depending on the purpose of the group, task groups can be empowering for the members of the group and/or the school culture, providing concrete evidence illustrating the direct efforts of the group. For example, a director of school counseling may form a task group and partner with building administrators (principal and vice principals) to prepare a presentation for the upcoming school board committee meeting that will showcase the impact and effect of a recent innovative program that was approved and implemented in the building. Possible outcomes of this task group can not only impact the working relationships of these essential building leaders, but also can have a ripple effect on the school culture, the students and/or families served by the program, and possibly the community as a whole, depending on the innovation and program. As the field of professional school counseling advocates for evidenced-based practices and data-driven innovations, school counselors can blend this push with the practical needs of the role.

From a broad level, we can identify many shared benefits and possible challenges with task groups regardless of which population may be engaging with or being served by the task group. Common benefits to task groups in schools include the following (note that this list is not exhaustive but rather representative of our experiences engaging in this type of work):

- *Adaptable*: Task groups can be short- or long-term; each group meeting can be brief in duration or held over an entire day as a workshop.
- *Flexible*: Task groups can focus on immediate here-and-now needs or on future planning. They can be used to evaluate past situations to inform a present or future need.
- *Inclusive*: They can provide a space for contributions from students, building staff, external stakeholders, and/or other essential individuals relevant or ancillary to the work of that group.
- *Versatile*: Task groups are versatile with regard to delivery mode or content focus. Virtual platforms and technological advances fuel collaborative opportunities with other schools, districts, and communities throughout the state and/or region, as well as nationally and/or internationally.

Challenges to planning or implementing task groups may include:

- *Logistics*. Schedules may not allow much, if any, flexible/free time during the school day, which may limit the frequency of when a group can meet. It may also unintentionally limit or exclude one or more persons.
- *Operational barriers*: Task groups may be formed in reaction to an unexpected need that could be internal to the school building or district or in reaction to a need issued from an external stakeholder (e.g., state education authority or federal requirement). If groups are rushed to be put together or the recommended group process is not used as part of the group, there may be unintended pitfalls that could impact finishing the task, transitioning, or identifying future roles and expectations of task groups.
- *Ambiguity*: Task groups that are hastily put together may impact the task itself that needs to be accomplished. Alternatively, the group leader's role or the goals and outcomes anticipated may be ambiguous. Therefore, members of the group will be unclear about their role or expectations for accomplishing the task.
- *Interpersonal concerns*: In a task group or any group, counterproductive interpersonal interactions stimulated by poor group leadership, mismatched leadership style and membership communication style, or other personality difficulties of individuals within the group could be a challenge to overcome.

Although task groups are most often used to help achieve their namesake—a specific task—they are also useful in a school setting to meet a variety of academic, social-emotional, and career-related needs. They may be formed to specifically address needs and goals of students, of teachers/staff, of administration, of parents, of counselors and support staff, or a broader community need. They may be formed for short-term needs to address an immediate issue or crisis or to identify a specific procedure or protocol to be used for a new service or requirement by the school district or the state or federal government. They may be formed for longer-term standing groups that will come together on a preset schedule or as needed to address related topics that may occur throughout the academic year. Let's separate our two critical audiences and explore how task groups can be used to support effective, evidenced-based, and dynamic work in the school setting.

Best practices in task groups consider all of the essential roles of the group—members and leaders. For groups to reach their optimal potential, the group as a whole system needs to be dynamically and actively functioning in adaptive ways. Recommendations for best practices are made available by the Association for Specialists in Group Work (ASGW) and are included Appendix B.

Task Groups as an Effective Approach for Children and Adolescents

Task groups often are applied in the context of here-and-now interaction, to promote efficient and effective accomplishment of group tasks, and to include members who are gathered to accomplish group task goals (DeLucia-Waack, 2006). Task groups with students in the school building may occur less often that those with adults, but they still invite a similar collaborative engagement to accomplish a specific goal or need under the supervision of one or more adults. Common examples of task groups throughout PreK-12 schools include student activity or academic clubs, parent–student meetings that may be with the counselor only or with a teacher as well, and student meetings with advocates or liaisons.

Using task groups with children and adolescents offers a number of benefits. One benefit is that the goals and objectives clearly communicate the expectations for the group. For example, because the goals and objectives are clearly spelled out, students are able to achieve success at accomplishing the tasks that are central to the group. Another benefit is that the students are able to learn skills within these groups that are transferable to other aspects of their lives, especially within the school setting. Teachers engage students with accomplishing tasks on a regular basis; participating in a task group as a member transfers to the classroom because students are able to make a connection between the activities they may be assigned and the larger task they are trying to accomplish. Another benefit of participating in a task group is seeing how individuals who are working collectively can build upon each other's strengths in order to accomplish a goal that would be beyond their ability to do in isolation.

Although there are many benefits to using task groups with children and adolescents, there are some important challenges to consider. First, depending on the child's stage of development, they may not be interested in working collectively on a project. This is important to consider because all students don't move through developmental stages at the same pace. Second, some children are more likely to voice their opinions than others, whereas others need more time to process information. Within a task group, it can be challenging to balance the different personalities as they relate to the task at hand. Along these lines, when taking race, ethnicity, gender, and other intersections of identity into account, some students may be less inclined to voice their opinion based on who else is in the group. For example, a seventh-grade African American girl who is on student council made up of a racially and culturally heterogeneous mixture of boys and girls might feel uncomfortable dissenting with the group when deciding whether nonconforming-gender bathrooms should be added to the school. Finally, engaging students in task groups can either be seen as great fun or total boredom. Some students respond really well to working together on a task, whereas others find it more difficult to stay committed. It will be important for the leader to help create an environment that is conducive to seeing the task through to the end. Working to create an enjoyable climate and constantly checking in with the students can help eliminate this challenge.

Task Groups as an Effective Approach for Adults in the School System

Task groups occur daily in the school building and are a cornerstone of collaborative engagement to accomplish the needs for all roles. Common examples of task groups throughout Prek-12 schools include leadership team planning meetings, response to intervention or special education screening team meetings, department/grade-level team meetings, and parent–teacher conferences.

Strategies that may help the counselor or group leader are to infuse structure, increasing as appropriate with the topic; to have a timeline to complete the work; and to have existing knowledge about the developmental level of the group members. When possible, having clear goals and expectations that are grounded in behaviors may also assist the group leader, especially if they are operating on a very short timeline. Leaders may consider using the SMART goal framework to identify the behavioral goals of the task group, with SMART standing for **S**pecific, **M**easurable, **A**chievable (or **A**ttainable), **R**ealistic (or **R**elevant), and **T**ime-oriented (or **T**imebound). This framework can be used to set short- or long-term objectives or goals. The exact origins of the SMART goal framework are not well documented, but appears to be most often credit Doran (1981 as cited in Day & Tosey, 2011) as well as appear in literature within the business, project management, and performance-planning sectors in the United States during the late 1970s and early 1980s (Day & Tosey, 2011). When you consider that the primary question is "How do you write a meaningful objective or goal?" the versatility of this framework shines bright. This framework is especially helpful in school settings due to the user-friendliness of its application to the needs of children and adults. It offers a common language that is centered on evidenced-based practices adaptable to different scenarios and developmental levels of the individual or group involved. It is a common framework used to support children and their families when writing goals as a part of an Individualized Educational Plan (IEP) or other accommodation services (e.g., 504) that may be applicable for a student in support of their equitable access to a free public education (see Table 5.1). While we can easily see how this framework can help to guide individual student or staff goals, the use of SMART goals was a key component to helping building-level task groups and even state-level task groups engage in a competitive federal grant opportunity in the United States in the early 2000s.

Supported by the American Recovery and Reinvestment Act, President Barack Obama and Secretary of Education Arne Duncan announced in the summer of 2009 a new competitive grant opportunity available to U.S. states and territories to ignite the state education and local district PreK-12 communities. The unique and aptly named competitive grant was Race to the Top (RTTT). States, the District of Columbia, and the Commonwealth of Puerto Rico were all invited to participate. The state education authority of the state/district/territory, in collaboration with participating school districts and buildings, was challenged to collaboratively identify comprehensive programming and accountability strategies that would meet the needs of their educational school improvement needs by capitalizing on their existing resources and obtaining new resources, if awarded this grant. The four primary areas of reform that were delineated by the U.S. Department of Education to yield school improvement outcomes via the RTTT grant project included:

- Adopting internationally benchmarked standards and assessments that prepare students for success in college and the workplace;
- Recruiting, developing, retaining, and rewarding effective teachers and principals, especially where they are needed most;
- Building data systems that measure student success and inform teachers and principals about how they can improve instruction; and
- Turning around our lowest-achieving schools (U.S. Department of Education, 2009).

By August 2010, 11 U.S. states and the District of Columbia had passed the first two phases of the grant program and had received awards. The next year competition open to those who were already actively participating took the bar higher by zeroing in on strategies for supporting efforts to leverage comprehensive statewide reform while also improving science, technology, engineering, and mathematics (STEM) education (U.S. Department of Education, 2011). In December, 2011, seven states received awards from phase three of the RTTT program. For all three phases of this federal grant, the use of task groups helped bring together state education authorities, local districts, and other community stakeholders. Applications submitted to the U.S. Department of Education utilized a variety of SMART goals to identify objectives and goals for success related to each state's comprehensive plan. The use of task groups and an intentional framework to identify and execute objectives and goals proved to be an efficient and effective strategy for several states that chose to take part in this national competition.

A common challenge within task groups as we consider some of the foundational elements that support effective group work is the very limited time to build and foster cohesion among the members of the group (Upton & Dagley, 2014). If there are acronyms or common language for a specialized field, and not all members share that same working knowledge or depth of it, then factions may unintentionally be created or some members may feel excluded from the group. Instances of role ambiguity or confusion may arise as prescreening and discussion of group norms, rules, and expectations may be limited or overlooked in many task groups. This may also extend to observable differences among members as to the purpose, goals, and targeted outcomes that the group is striving for. It may also be likely that in a task group, one or two members may take more of the reins in discussions or actions, effectively monopolizing a group, inviting a negative group dynamic.

TABLE 5.1   Format for Writing SMART Goals With Examples and Nonexamples

Nonexamples	Examples
Given instructional reading-level text, Eugenia will increase her oral reading rate by 22 words correct per minute.	Given a Guided Reading Level S passage, individualized reading instruction in word chunking and use of context, and directions to read quickly and smoothly, Eugenia will read aloud with 95% accuracy at a rate of 84 words correct per minute in two of three trials by [target date].
When asked, Maverick will brush his teeth with 100% accuracy.	When provided the appropriate materials (i.e., a toothbrush, toothpaste, and sink) and prompted to brush, Maverick will brush his teeth after school snack or meal time, completing 8 of 10 steps independently, 4 days per week for 3 consecutive weeks [target date].
Given a grade-level math CBM, Jorge will score 31 problems correct.	Given a third-grade mixed-operation math computation CBM, pencil and paper, and the prompt to work for 8 minutes, Jorge will solve and write the answers with 31 problems correct in three consecutive trials by [target date].

Note: CBM = curriculum-based measure; IEP = Individualized Education Program.
Source: Hedin, L. & DeSpain, S. (2018). SMART or not? Writing specific and measurable IEP goals. *Teaching Exceptional Children, 51*(2), 100–110. https://doi-org.libproxy.lib.unc.edu/10.1177/0040059918802587

   The essential formula of the SMART goal integrates identified conditions, observable and concrete behaviors, with a clear goal and date of completion. The formula compiles several variables into one declarative sentence that can be answered with a "yes" or "no" response when asked if the goal has been completed, achieved, or reached. The formula is versatile to adapt to any developmental level of a person, any culture or language background, and any type of topic. We see in Table 5.1 how this is applied in a classroom setting for a teacher working with students. This same formula can easily be translated to the work counselors will do on academic, social-emotional, or career goals with students from the PreK–12 levels. It can also be a common language used when counselors collaborate with teachers and families as an interactive support for the learner.

This can also occur very quickly and sometimes unexpectedly if a leader is on a tight timeline or overloaded with too many responsibilities, limiting focus on the group process itself. Upton and Dagly (2014) offered example language that a counselor or group leader may consider sharing as a part of a group's first meeting to help clarify expectations and begin creating the space for inclusionary collaboration within the group: "It may be easy at times to have one or two members accept all responsibility for contributing thoughts and ideas, relative to our task, but we need comments and assistance from each, so let's help each other contribute" (p. 29).

Culturally Relevant and Ethically Sound Application of the TRATE My Group Framework

T – Building from the section above integrating task groups as an effective approach for adults in the schools, the **Type** of group used is a task group. The purpose of the task group will be to work with school staff on creating culturally relevant instructional strategies that can be measured with clear objective behaviors expected. Often, input from the entire leadership team including building-level and district administration can be a helpful starting place to identify desired outcomes. From there, the task group can fill in the other elements of the SMART goal formula or other goal strategies that will be used. Typically, each school is tasked with identifying and implementing the culturally relevant instruction recognizing each school community is unique.

R – The **Role(s)** the leader(s) will play is to communicate clearly the goals and objectives from the district level to the school staff while being intentional about creating an environment conducive to discussing how these goals can be applied in their unique school setting. The leader(s) will need to balance accomplishing the tasks at hand with leaving room for the important discussions that may arise. The leader(s) will also need to teach and model giving and receiving feedback for the participants. Based on the goals and objectives being established by the district, the leader(s) will need to be both vulnerable and honest in order to buffer any resistance that may arise within the group. The role the staff will take or hold could present in the following manner. Due to the sensitivity of the topic and the fear of being misunderstood, some staff may choose to remain quiet. Other staff may be defensive or angry because the leader(s) of the task group is not a teacher, or, depending on their intersection of identities, may be assumed as less knowledgeable on the topic. Some staff may be champions or allies to this specific cause. It is important to note that the leader(s) should be on the lookout for the various roles that the staff may take.

A – The **Audience** first and foremost are the teachers themselves who have been directly impacted by these administrative mandates. Teachers will be on the front lines implementing any changes offered within the curriculum. Other ancillary audience include the stakeholders that might not be present but would be invested in the group's success such as the students, school support staff, and families. The impetus for this task is coming from outside of the school, therefore being sensitive to the staff members will be very important.

T - The **Timeline** of the groups will depend on the scheduling of the group, the projected schedule, and session details such as start and ending times. In this case, the groups will need time to communicate to the school-level staff, students, and families the charge of modifying the curriculum in a manner that aims to be more inclusive and excellent. If the group leaders are charged to complete this task in rapid fashion due to the urgency of the request, it will be important to balance the outside pressure with the realities of the stakeholders within the school. The schedule of this type of group could be weekly meetings in person or virtually. The sessions should not be shorter than 1 hour at a time and ideally would be 1 hour and 10 minutes to provide time to process the information. The number of sessions is constrained by the school calendar, but task groups are more effective if they aim for as many meetings needed to establish strong group cohesion and an environment conducive to productivity (Yalom & Leszcz, 2020). The longer the task group meets, the higher the chances for success.

E - The **Expected outcomes** or goals for this task group focused on comprehensively infusing culturally relevant teaching strategies across the curriculum will take a concerted effort. The task group meetings will need a clear broad goal and specific objectives to provide a platform for the participants to generate pedagogical strategies for the teachers and other support staff to build on their current expertise. Additionally, identifying areas that school staff can improve upon in this endeavor is also important, and the task group may conclude with just accomplishing the creation of other areas for improvement in the future. The primary objectives of this task group will be to identify the strengths, agency, champions for this initiative, and areas for improvement. The secondary objectives will be to develop a plan for employing the best strategies to implement these culturally relevant strategies within the school. Finally, the last potential objective will be to examine a plan for communicating the process and steps for following up. The broad goal and specific objectives at the onset will need to be generated very early in the process. They will also need to be clear, concise, and attainable. Using the SMART goal framework to structure the goal and objectives is one user-friendly manner to provide clarity on the charge of the task group. The group leader can also be attuned to the group process as things unfold, but the task group is less malleable due to the nature of the work.

Pulling It All Together

In this chapter, we discussed task groups and the ways in which they can be used with students and adults in a school setting. The major emphasis was on how school counselors can use a task group to bring adults together to address important concerns that might impact students, staff, families, and other important stakeholders. Concrete goal-setting formulas and frameworks, such as SMART goals, is one way to achieve this inviting engagement from all adults and school personnel. Topics that can be addressed by adults through the use of task groups are endless. Based on recent trends, some common topics have included, but are not limited to: suicide ideation, mental health, social emotional learning, and school engagement versus singularly focusing on student achievement. In sum, task groups will be another tool school counselors can use to manage school staff, crisis teams, and department heads, and other school leaders at meeting the mental health needs of students and teachers. School counselors can use their skills and talents to offer group spaces for both practical and health-related outcomes.

DISCUSSION QUESTIONS

1. What stands out as the most salient contribution of task groups to a school environment?

2. School counselors can use task groups to address mental health concerns. What could be a goal of this type of group? What would be the objective? Who would be the audience?

3. The authors suggest that the more group sessions the better; what stands out to you about this recommendation? What are some pros and cons to running endless task groups?

4. As a school counselor, what might be some barriers to facilitating task groups when teachers and school staff are the members?

REFERENCES

Day, T. &. Tosey, P. (2011). Beyond SMART? A new framework for goal setting. *The Curriculum Journal, 22*(4), 515-534.

DeLucia-Waack, J. L. (2006). Leading psychoeducational groups for children and adolescents. SAGE Publications.

Hedin, L. & DeSpain, S. (2018). SMART or not? Writing specific and measurable IEP goals. *Teaching Exceptional Children, 51*(2), 100–110. https://doi-org.libproxy.lib.unc.edu/10.1177/0040059918802587

Schumacher, R. A., & Ache, L. (2014). Collaboration with administration and teachers: Developing value and support for classroom guidance. In J. DeLucia-Waack (Ed.), *School counselors share their favorite classroom guidance lessons: A guide to choosing, planning, conducting, and processing* (pp. 13–24). Association for Specialists in Group Work.

Upton, A. W., & Dagley, J. C. (2014). Leadership principles for classroom guidance lessons as a task group. In J. DeLucia-Waack (Ed.), *School counselors share their favorite classroom guidance lessons: A guide to choosing, planning, conducting, and processing* (pp. 25–32). Association for Specialists in Group Work.

U.S. Department of Education. (2009, December). *Race to the Top.* https://www2.ed.gov/programs/race-tothetop/factsheet.html

U.S. Department of Education. (2011, December 23). Department of Education awards $200 million to seven states to advance K-12 reform. Press release. https://www.ed.gov/news/press-releases/department-education-awards-200-million-seven-states-advance-k-12-reform

Yalom, I. D., & Leszcz, M. (2020). *The theory and practice of group psychotherapy.* Basic Books.

Working With Families and Other Stakeholders That Impact Schools and Districts

Students are not the only key stakeholder that a school counselor's work will impact on a daily basis. Every day school counselors engage in meaningful collective tasks with families on behalf of their children using a group work framework. Identifying useful group leadership and facilitation skills when collaborating with families can promote the power of group dimensions regardless of the particular content, situation, or participants involved. Evidence of universality, cohesion, and/or interpersonal learning (see Chapter 2) observed through process and/or outcome factors are expected when effective group dynamics and leadership are in place. Stretching the group leadership skills and perspective to include the intentional collaborative and interpersonal dynamics when working with families and other adult stakeholders has implications for those relationships as well as the ongoing work counselors have with the student(s). Opportunities for intrapersonal and interpersonal communication and social and emotional learning and development for children, adolescents, and their families are abundant.

Foundational Knowledge, Contextual Dimensions, and Practice

The objectives for this chapter are as follows:

1. Understand collaboration models that inform school counseling.
2. Identify theoretical foundations that support working with families in a group setting.
3. Maintain the student/child as the center of services, meeting the needs of children through their families.
4. Describe the social and emotional learning (SEL) model.

School counselors are well aware that collaboration is an essential skill embedded within their training and preparation programs, yet it is impossible to fully conceive what opportunities will emerge in schools that capitalize on this training in collaboration. *Collaboration* is the process of two or more people working in concert to successfully accomplish something that is significant and relevant for people within and beyond the collaborative relationship (Baker et al., 2009). Another helpful definition the American School Counselor Association (ASCA) offers embedded within the National Model (2019) is that collaboration is any meeting between two or more individuals working toward a single goal, and/or working with other educators, parents, and the community to support student achievement and to advocate for equity and access for all students (Brigman et al., 2018). Specifically, this means working collectively with students, staff, families, and others to make a positive impact on students and their families. Some might suggest that this is better defined as *consultation*, or that these words are even interchangeable (Brigman et al., 2018). To ensure clarity of understanding we use the term *collaboration* because it implies that school counselors are deeply involved with the process, whereas *consultation* could result in work being conducted on the periphery or a different distribution of balance, responsibilities, or role expectations among the parties involved. Consultation can often be misinterpreted as an "expert advice" experience, which is not the intention we are suggesting to intentionally integrate group leadership skills with collaboration skills. Collaboration skills are instrumental in every aspect of a school counselor's job because of the many students, teachers, administrators, families, and community members served. Successful collaborative efforts will entail school counselors using their group leadership skills to produce great results.

School counselors must be intentional about accepting and acknowledging that all of the people involved in the collaborative operations will react in a number of ways to different people. In fact, some families of color may hesitate to participate in school activities, especially if their own school experiences were negative or even traumatic (Cook et al., 2020). Some families may be perceived as being resistant to participating, but it may actually be a lack of awareness or understanding of how a school activity may be beneficial to the entire family system. The caution is just because "things have always been done that way" in the school building does not mean that all of the families and students who cycle through the building and district understand or are aware. By tapping into our group leadership skills, we remain aware of the multitude of perspectives from diverse stakeholder groups being served by our work on a daily basis. This intentional and reflective awareness, enhanced by direct actions taken attending to inclusive opportunities, will guard against complacency or exclusive behaviors. Although it is critical to create inviting environments for families and their children within schools, sometimes a concerted effort will need to be made to ensure broad diversity within the school populations are considered and included when decisions for practice are made. Again, data-informed practice will increase the chances of collaboration efforts targeting salient concerns for all students and families. This forward thinking and awareness will help to maximize the support offered to students and families, particularly those who may justifiably be skeptical about the intentions of those leading school-related efforts or due to their own difficult experiences faced in schools (Laurea & Horvat, 1999).

Successful collaborative endeavors consist of participants who all play a role or see themselves as important pieces during the process or event. Helping members identify and access their value is no small matter, and could help reap big results. Strategic, clear, and forward-thinking leadership skills that foster an environment where all voices are heard will set a stage that lends itself to productive and fulfilling results within any number of collective tasks or events.

THINK ABOUT IT ... LET'S REFLECT

- Have you ever been on a sports team or part of a Girl Scout troop, mission team, or event planning team? What about a team that was filled with people you have never met? How racially, culturally or ethnically diverse were these teams?

- Reflect on how different each of these teams were, including demographics, leadership behavior, and dispositions, and how outcomes unfolded over time. How intentionally were the participants' culture(s) acknowledged? To what extent were all voices valued?

- What part did you play in the planning (pregame or pre-event), implementation (game, event, or action) and evaluation/reflection (postgame or postevent) of the tasks/goals, and to what extent were the goals accomplished? How influential were your ideas along the way?

- What is the most salient aspect that stands out to you at each of these stages (e.g., before, during or after) for this example in your mind? What stands out as the biggest challenge, fear, or concern you may have had before, during, or after the event? As you reflect, recall specifically how race and culture were viewed in terms of strengths and/or deficits.

- What did you anticipate as being a concern for disrupting the anticipated goals and outcomes that either were never addressed or failed to materialize? What individual or group of persons received the most credit for the success or ill success of the project? How did the team address racial or cultural biases that may have been present?

Theoretical Foundations to Support Working With Families in a Group Setting

Another way to contextualize and build collaborative supportive environments is to consider the various roles family members play in the lives of their children and to harness this support for their students' success. Families are a subsystem that impacts a student's experience within and outside of the school environment. School counselors and adults within the school can apply basic elements from different foundational family therapy orientations to target the current needs and environments within schools. The following paragraphs discuss two formative contributors to family therapy, Salvador Minunchin and Virginia Satir. We highlight foundational tenets from their respective approaches, and stretch further to adapt and apply school–family collaborative partnerships with the TRATE My Group framework.

Salvador Minunchin is a well-regarded contributor among strategic family therapists. School counselors are aided in their work by drawing on some of the key assumptions and concepts from this lens as they consider collaborative efforts with families. Strategic family influences include (Minuchin & Fishman, 1981; Minunchin et al., 2006):

- The brief and time-limited approach
- The cognitive-behavioral and solution-brief theoretical orientations commonly used among school counselors

- A problem-centered focus with an emphasis on "the process"
- Clever, creative, innovative, prescriptive, and practical perspectives and interventions that aim to identify and support modifications to the families behavioral interactions

One of the basic principles in strategic family therapy that fuels the TRATE My Group framework is that people are always communicating. The messages communicated may be overt, covert, clearly understood by a receiver as intended by the deliverer, or misunderstood. An inherent responsibility of school counselors, regardless of the topic, is to assist and guide those who they work to engage in effective communication. Through clear and adaptive communication, intra- and interpersonal growth and change become possible. This strategic emphasis on accurate communication expands the possibility of inclusivity; a cultural perspective of customs, traditions, values, and beliefs is a necessary component to be included if the family, group, or system invites it. Without clear communication, individuals and groups of individuals are susceptible to dysfunction and maladaptive thoughts, feelings, and/or behaviors.

Virginia Satir is regarded as the "mother" of experiential family therapy and is known for her human validation process model (Brothers, 2011). The validation process model centralizes communication patterns as the core of affective self-esteem, self-worth, and interpersonal relationships. Satir's contributions emerged around the same time as those of another well-recognized psychotherapist, Carl Rogers, who shared the perspective of genuineness, authenticity, and positive regard among interpersonal relationships as being essential to supporting growth and change (Brothers, 2011). Satir believed that (1) all people are inherently good and have the innate ability to change and grow as they need to (2) people may need support and assistance to discover and guide them along the way.

Regardless of a school counselor's view of human nature, a universal assumption among practitioners in the field is that adaptive growth and change is possible. The main culprits for disrupting the growth and change process for individuals, groups, or a system are low self-esteem, low self-worth, and dysfunctional or destructive communication patterns, to name a few. Within school settings, external factors, including racism, oppression, microaggressions, and stereotypes, can interfere with successful development (Delgado & Stefancic, 2001; Solorzano, 1998; Yosso et al., 2009). Satir's human validation process model offers a guide for counselors' work to increase students and families' self-esteem, self-worth, and self-concept and to reach congruent communication patterns within the system while encouraging empathy in order to create the environment the individual(s) need to access their own inner strength and capabilities for healing, growth, and change (Guth et al., 2019).

It is easy to see the relevance of the components of the two family theories mentioned above for the work of a school counselor when parent meetings occur, with or without the child involved. School counselors foster school–family relationships and collaborations in order to promote their students' academic success by recognizing that several factors impact children's ability to be successful in the school. Expanding these models to incorporate community building will take more intentionality, especially as the need to strengthen and engage the broader community is concerned (Guth et al., 2019).

Adapting some of the foundational elements gleaned from Minunchin and Satir will help to inform a school counselor's practice, especially when working with collaborative groups. For instance, counselors can prioritize adaptive communication, create an environment that supports growth- and strength-based perspectives, and process the interactions by valuing the voices that are participating and advocating on behalf of the voices that are not represented (Kervick et al., 2020). All of these efforts transfer to a logistical setting that is time limited and adaptable for working with diverse groups. Other intentional strategies to consider in preparation for partnering with families and others from outside the school could include:

- Using semi-formal language that includes titles such as Mr., Ms., or Mrs. and last names until counselors have been invited to use first names or nicknames. Although the interaction within the school culture may utilize first names, often as part of White middle-class cultural norms, it may not be as easily transferable to other customs when working with families from diverse backgrounds.

- Ensuring that all families and students have clear understandings of the goals of each meeting, which may require multiple primer meetings or translators available for languages or concepts to increase the likelihood of clarity.

- Considering the mode and time of communication as a way of recognizing that not all families have schedules or occupations that can accommodate being available during typical business hours to participate; this does not mean that they are not interested to be involved, and exploring possibilities for evening, early morning, or virtual communications and meetings is appropriate.

- Counselors are reminded that racial, cultural, and ethnic backgrounds influence the perspective a child and their caretakers could have when interacting with school personnel. Counselors must be especially sensitive when working with undocumented immigrant students and their caretakers (Davidson & Burson, 2017). For example, state education authorities, school district administration, and/or building-level administrators and other school personnel involved in the registration process for a new student hold positions of power and authority. It will be important to remember that previous experiences with education systems could influence how the student and/or family are engaging in the process now in your school.

- Asking thoughtful questions to gain insight and build rapport with the family and students. This effort helps to demonstrate a respect of the cultural and family background and an interest in getting to know the unique characteristics of those families involved. It will require a concerted effort to understand the value of the person's culture for the individual and the family regarding their nuclear and extended family; their view of collectivism; how they are engaged with the various communities in their world; what their customs are around food, dates, the role of time, and interpersonal interactions; and how communication occurs, both verbally and nonverbally (Lorie et al., 2017; Singh et al., 2020).

- Evaluating experiences, biases, assumptions, and areas of awareness and modeling for students and others that we are all unique people, each with a unique story. Seeking consultation and supervision, when needed, supports the continued growth and development of a professional counselor (Brigman et al., 2018).

School counselors work to help families from a myriad of racial and cultural backgrounds to recognize their strengths. School counselors are intentional about understanding how powerful accurate and inclusive communication can be on a system. School counselors use their knowledge of collaboration, family dynamics, and comprehensive developmental frameworks to meet the needs of families from all walks of life. The social and emotional learning model is an important part of successful schools. Understanding this concept and its application to strong collaborative partnerships affords a unique opportunity to meet the needs of families.

Social and Emotional Learning (SEL) Model Applied to Families

The social and emotional learning (SEL) model is a comprehensive strengths-based developmental framework that can help students and their families participate in successful and engaging interpersonal encounters (Greenberg et al., 2017). Specifically, the SEL model underscores the imperative that learning is embedded within relationships and that students and families express themselves based on personal experiences within schools as students and parents. These ongoing encounters experienced by students and families will influence the educational environments in which new skills are taught or learned and the interactions and exchanges of knowledge that emerge in reference to one's self, worldview, family, community, and so forth. Simply put, one's social and emotional capital influences the extent to which their hearts and minds are open.

SEL advocates believe that:

- Social and emotional competencies can be modeled and practiced in ways that foster positive student, teacher, school staff, and family interactions.
- Positive and collaborative relationships between students, teachers, school staff, and families increase chances for success within school and beyond.
- Improvement in students' social and emotional skills, which can be taught, discussed and reflected upon, impacts one's attitudes, relationships, academic performance, and perceptions of the classroom and school climate.
- Interventions within schools have led to long-term social and emotional skill improvement and performance in the classroom.

Schools can create conditions that foster a willingness and commitment to learn with and from one another in order to build on all of the unique collaborative opportunities with the relevant stakeholders. School counselors can be instrumental in facilitating environments of collaboration that empower students and families to benefit from intentionally supportive and productive group interactions (Bryan & Henry, 2012; Cook et al., 2020; Cohen, 2006). School counselors who understand the SEL model and its benefits will be better suited to engage students, school staff, and families in collaborative enterprises.

The benefits summarized by researchers within the SEL model are the acquisition and application of knowledge, skills, and attitudes to develop healthy identities, manage emotions, and achieve personal and collective goals (Devaney & Berg, 2016; Durlak et al., 2011). Furthermore, the SEL model helps people feel and show empathy for others, establish and maintain supportive relationships, and make responsible and caring decisions. The essential interconnectedness and awareness of others within the SEL framework overlaps cleanly with the foundational tenets of the TRATE My Group framework and general group leadership skills. This intersectionality and overlap can support smoother applications and direct efforts to employ SEL perspectives when engaging in TRATE My Group work.

SEL guidance benefits the genuine school–family-community partnerships built on these underlying principles to foster trusting and collaborative relationships, rigorous and meaningful curriculum and instruction, and ongoing evaluation of the teaching and learning experiences. Young people and adults can be inspired to cocreate thriving schools and contribute to safe, healthy, and just communities. School counselors are well prepared to use group leadership skills to devise strategies that work in schools and benefit all those involved in collaborative endeavors. The ultimate goal is to ensure that all students and their families have the opportunity for general well-being.

Put another way, school counselors also often focus on schoolwide initiatives. These endeavors may include fostering positive, caring, and empowering school and community climates. There is no doubt that schoolwide change can impact a wider number of students and families. Essentially, school counselors can use their unique skills to facilitate training, collaborative meetings, and interventions with students, families, and staff to create school and community environments that build on the strengths of the participants (Brigman et al., 2018).

Culturally Relevant and Ethically Sound Application of the TRATE My Group Framework

Numerous important topics or problems for debate or discussion emerge within schools that could impact family and community members. For instance, creating a college-going culture within a school could have long-term benefits to the community given that a strong workforce is built on a strong educational foundation. In the 21st century, postsecondary options (e.g., trade school, community college, university attendance, and so forth) can increase the capital available within the community. *College-going culture* refers to the environment, attitudes, and practices in schools and communities that encourage students and families to obtain the information, tools, and perspectives to enhance access to and success in postsecondary education (McClafferty Jarsky et al., 2009). Important considerations include linking interventions and program efforts across the PreK-12 continuum. For instance, elementary school students can begin to gain an understanding of options for their futures and the background and knowledge (e.g., education) required for certain careers. The middle school years can help to gain a deeper focus on these educational requirements. Along the way, schools in both elementary and middle school settings can engage in honest discussions with students and their families as to what it takes to prepare for postsecondary education. As the transition occurs to high school, students and families can be exposed to environments that are collaborative in building school, family, and community partnerships that reinforce the same message of high expectations for a student's future. Duly noted are the fears and concerns that many students and families may have about funding their college hopes and dreams. School counselors fostering college-going environments will also work to validate these concerns and generate realistic solutions and strategies to mitigate these fears (McDonough, 2004).

Another critical and controversial topic is the *school-to-prison pipeline*. The school-to-prison pipeline is initiated when a student gets in serious trouble at school and there is law enforcement within the building to compel compliance with zero-tolerance policies (Gregory et al., 2010). This student's contact with the criminal justice system is profound and oftentimes the consequences are more severe for Black and Hispanic males. The school, in this case, can become a pipeline to prison for these students who are punished in ways that may treat them as budding criminals. In other words, when a school allows school personnel (e.g., a resource officer) to arrest a student or mandates, as a consequence to an infraction, a student to be referred to law enforcement or a juvenile court system, the impact on that student (child or adolescent) can alter their life course dramatically.

The school-to-prison pipeline disrupts the potential for healthy communities and particularly impacts African American and Hispanic boys within school settings. For instance, even as early as preschool African American children represent 18% of preschool enrollment but 48% of pre-school children receiving more than one out-of-school suspension. In comparison, White students represent 43% of preschool enrollment but only 26% of preschool children receiving more than one out-of-school suspension. In terms of the discrepancy when comparing races, PreK-12 schools have disproportionately high suspension/expulsion rates for students of color. Specifically, African American students are suspended and expelled at a rate three times greater than White students; on average, 5% of White students are suspended, compared to 16% of African American students. When it comes to arrests and referrals to law enforcement by race and disability status, the statistics are just as disconcerting: African American students represent 16% of student enrollment within public schools but comprise 27% of the students referred to law enforcement and 31% of students subjected to a school-related arrest. In comparison, 41% of students referred to law enforcement and 39% of those arrested are White, even though White students represent approximately 51% of enrollment in public schools (Darensbourg et al., 2010).

Other concerns that often emerge during adolescence and young adulthood that may impact family and community members include family transitions, such as the addition of new family members (e.g., sibling or step parent); deployment of a parent serving in the armed forces; or parental unemployment. Families and communities also may be affected by suicide, gang activity, or other tragedies, including human trafficking. Working with families affected by these issues to deeply understand their collective needs can be accomplished using different group formats. Below we provide a selection of examples to illustrate initiatives that could be developed and offer an example of the application of the TRATE My Group framework. The examples will require interpersonal, collaboration, leadership, and systematic thinking skills. School counselors acquire these skills during their master's preparation as well as on the job through trial and error. To briefly illustrate, imagine that there is a leaky faucet in your kitchen. You would have a sense of urgency to fix the leak rather than covering it up. This goal of fixing the faucet is to avoid wasting water, and therefore extraneous costs. In the case of groups, involving family members in school settings will require an intentionality with leveling the language used in communication, inspiring group thinking, creating flexible solution-solving, and investigating issues that stand to change the school and surrounding community.

Consider the following case illustration as a way to offer more clarity on the power of groups and the usefulness of the TRATE My Group framework. Imagine that a school administrator approached the school counseling team about a major concern that has emerged within the community and school and on social media. Additionally, imagine that this concern is so far-reaching that staff (i.e., coaches) and some students, particularly those who received the threats and other students of color, as well as some families, are seeking help to deal with racial conflict that was initiated outside of the school. Specifically, following winter break and culminating the weekend before the Martin Luther King holiday, empty nooses were hung downtown at some of the local businesses, Confederate flags were taped to the front of the school building and football field, and anonymous threats and violent references to students of color surfaced on different social medial tags. The school administration, school counseling department, and athletic staff met as a leadership team to discuss how to address this growing racial conflict. Following these brainstorming meetings, the counseling department offered to create a program that would stimulate grassroots efforts to eradicate the racist messaging emerging on social media and in the community concerning the conflict and hostile school environments. One creative intervention found within the scholarly literature, referred to as a racial dialogues, could be instrumental in offering members of the community the chance to discuss their past and/or present experiences with race and racism within a particular school environment and surrounding community (Cook et al., 2020). Racial dialogues are also referred to as *courageous conversations* or *intergroup dialogues.*

Fundamentally, these types of learning environments are based on critical race theory, which asserts five important tenets. First, race and racism is all around us and intersects with other types of oppression. Second, it is necessary to challenge and dismantle educational practices and race-neutral policies. Third, an emphasis on social justice advocacy to empower minoritized communities is emphasized. Fourth, sharing of narratives help participants understand the stories of others who have participated in or suffered from racism and oppression. Fifth, the necessity of understanding the dynamics of power and oppression and the role played to reduce inequities in education (Delgado & Stefancic, 2001; Solorzano, 1998; Yosso et al., 2009).

Although there is a limited amount of evidence on the benefits of participants' involvement in racial dialogues, they have been found to offer support for one's personal well-being, community building, honesty, and collaboration with individuals from all walks of life for a small sample of adults (e.g., parents and school staff). However, a number of difficulties have been identified, including time limitations and wavering commitment of the participants (Cook et al., 2020). The ultimate goal of racial dialogue is to dissect the school and community climate and to foster educational justice. In the example we dissect below, the focus includes raising awareness about the recent racial tension and engaging in a game plan for action.

> **T** – The **Type**. Racial dialogues can be used as part of a task group, counseling group, or psychoeducational group. As a task group, the meetings would aim to accomplish the goal of creating a more inclusive school environment with the help of different school and community stakeholders. Racial dialogues could also be used as small group interventions (e.g., counseling) or large group interventions (e.g., psychoeducational). If used as interventions, the goal will focus mainly on those who are actually participants, whereas a task group may have a more far-reaching influence, with participants engaging in both raising awareness about the present concerns and also coming up with strategies to combat racism throughout the school and community. In this example, the specific purpose of this group work is to promote racial awareness that is specific and targeted within these particular

environments. Following this growing awareness, the focus can shift to community fostered action and change initiatives. The research on effectiveness of such programs is limited, but the emerging findings are promising (Cook et al., 2020).

R – The **Role.** These task groups will have a number of leaders, and, the roles they play will vary based on the type of group. For this example, the group leaders hosting a racial dialogue task group will need to consider both immediate plans and ongoing strategies, because this type of racial tension will not be put to rest easily. The specific role the leaders will play will include engaging participants in reviewing tentative goals that offer a place to discuss what has been witnessed or experienced in various situations and community building through honest discussions. Group leaders will need to consider how to help participants overcome any barriers such as fear, hesitation, or skepticism that may percolate before, during, or even after the sessions.

The participants' roles include offering feedback on the identified goals, responding to prompts and dialogue stimuli, and generating ideas to address specific concerns recognized both within the group and outside of the group. It is important to note that participants will need opportunities to explore any concerns they may have.

A – The **Audience** will include stakeholders such as the students themselves, both those who have been directly and indirectly impacted by these racist actions; families and community members; and school faculty and staff. The audience will not all participate in the task groups, but the outcomes that are targeted will aim to help both school and community members who are endowed in the group's success, but in this case the audience also includes those who could be less steeped in successful engaged community efforts. For example, this task group will deal directly with racial tension that has been spreading via social media and also around town in the school and community. The major disgruntlement gleaned from the tactics used suggest a resentment for the number of immigrants moving into the area from different countries, resistance to the Black Lives Matter fervor reignited by recent episodes of police brutality throughout the United States, interracial dating, and fear of the implications of fostering more "inclusive" environments viewed as overcompensating for students and families of color. Therefore it is duly noted that the audience spans both for those in favor of such work and those who are the perpetrators.

T – The **Timeline** of the racial dialogue task group includes the planning of the actual sessions. The timeline includes the schedule and session details such as start and ending times, length of the meetings, and follow up and other considerations for long-term engagement. Time constraints that may impact leaders or members as well as sustaining passion, action, and commitment will need to be acknowledged in order to increase opportunities for successful outcomes.

E – The **Expected outcomes**, also referred to as the *goals*, include providing a space to engage in difficult conversations about the realities that many students, families, and staff are facing as a result of the heightened racial tension surfacing throughout the school and community. Another goal, following the discussions that will expose the realities participants and stakeholders are facing, is to cocreate specific action items that can address the pernicious environments resulting from the overt symbols of racism and discrimination. Goals that might arise over time are yet to be determined, but could include establishing spaces for both victims and culprits to engage in honest discussions and come to agreements to disagree without causing additional harm whereby all voices are respected and all people are accepted despite one's race or ethnic or cultural background. *The main purpose and expected outcomes include fostering educational justice by raising awareness about the recent racial tension and engaging in a plan for action.*

GROUPS IN ACTION

Now, using the TRATE My Group framework, example scenarios are provided below, along with suggested process and content questions. Reflect and generate ideas for applying the TRATE My Group framework to one of the scenarios.

Example 1: A mother contacts the school because she has a set of twin daughters who attend your school. She has recently remarried and a new baby is on the way in the next year.

Example 2: A new student has recently enrolled in your school. A few days after his arrival, the family contacts you because their son has been cyberbullied and the nature of the bullying was racially motivated. The boy has recently arrived from Somalia, and due to his darker skin, he has been targeted with vulgar words typically used toward African Americans. Although this issue occurred outside of the school, it has begun to manifest itself in school because the boy feels less comfortable attending and is isolating himself during lunch, recess, and other extracurricular times.

Example 3: You have a strong female high school athlete who is also very academically oriented. She is interested in attending college to pursue an athletic career, but her long-term career goals are not clear. Additionally, this student has the opportunity to receive a partial athletic scholarship to compete at a mid-level Historically Black College or University (HBCU), but could likely receive more funding if she were to attend a more familiar and reputable Predominantly White Institution (PWI); however, she would have to give up the chance to play competitively in college because her athletic skill level doesn't match those expected at this particular PWI.

Suggested Process and Content Questions

- Which scenario did you choose, and what are some types of groups you could run?
- What role would you and the participants play? What skills and strategies could the leaders used to teach or gather important information?
- Identify and describe all of the parties who make up the audience?
- Describe the timeline and other scheduling factors (e.g., number of sessions, session length, days and times) that would be most appropriate for the group programs you chose.
- How many different expected outcomes (e.g., goals and objectives) were developed?

Groups-in-Action Activity: Possible Application

The following examples offer useful applications and expansion of the ideas presented above. To illustrate, we provide suggestions for hosting a workshop and facilitating a focus group(s) as additional ideas that could speak to the needs of the brainstorming discussed above.

Type – A psychoeducational group could be structured to create workshops for parents and teachers on student development issues. Some of the topics for these workshops could include bullying prevention, course selection, school competitions (e.g., scavenger hunts, spelling bees, or math events), and mentoring. Sometimes families need knowledge or skills about specific familial concerns, including the impact of disabilities, aging parents, blended families, or consequences of stress and anxiety due to unforeseen circumstances. It is not unusual for some urbanized schools serving poor students in less affluent districts to suffer from high teacher turnover. Therefore, workshops could integrate group counseling strategies and techniques to facilitate a critical discourse that includes an educational component concerning teacher retention issues. Group work and group systems thinking can help by creating goals and outcomes that include indicators for both student and teacher success. Facilitating a workshop that includes opportunities for teachers for their input toward barriers may provide specific suggestions that might otherwise be unknown about retaining these teachers in particular.

Along those lines, a type of task group could be created, referred to as a *focus group*, in a way that group-related skills can be employed. A *focus group* is generally defined as a group interview involving a small number of demographically similar or dissimilar people, depending on the purpose, that can be used for gauging needs of students, families, and/or staff by collecting information (e.g., data) to solve a problem, gain insight, or receive feedback on preliminary information. For example, a focus group could be used to help families provide genuine and honest insight on policy initiatives and changes thereafter. Offering spaces for families to share their voices creates inclusive environments that support culturally relevant curriculums and indigenous considerations and places spotlights on areas within the system that need attention. Focus groups can be designed in a manner to engage in face-to-face, virtual, or blended (e.g., in person and digitized formats) communication. More about technology is discussed in Chapter 7. Focus groups built using the TRATE My Group framework provide guidance on platform setup; facilitation, which allows the content/topic to shift anytime needed; and attention to the parallel process that unfolds as the group dynamics unfold.

Role – The role of a group leader within a workshop is likely to facilitate the delivery of information, process the understanding and reactions to this information, and offer resources for gathering more information on this topic. The role of a group leader within a focus group is to gather original data from selected participants. In some cases, whether for a workshop or focus group, the leaders can include school administrators, counselors, teachers, staff, family volunteers, or students. Skills include delivering knowledge and facilitating discussion using a structured or semi-structured interview protocol. Further, workshops and focus groups can promote broader and deeper understanding for leaders and participants about their current understanding, perceptions, or hopes and dreams regarding topics of concerns. In both workshops and focus groups, discussion prompts, basic group counseling skills (e.g., reflection of thoughts and feelings), self-disclosure, immediacy, and honesty are useful tools. Group techniques help to ensure that efficient partnerships are maintained and nurtured when serving stakeholders with workshops or gathering data in focus groups.

In both workshops and focus groups, the participants can include teachers and staff or a family member with or without their children in the same group. The role of the participants within the workshop is mainly to learn about a topic at hand, but can also include processing the information that is learned and offering feedback on what worked well along with general and specific areas for improvement. In contrast, focus groups are created for participants to share their feedback about the topic of discussion. For instance, participants might be asked to share their impressions of identified policies and practices that school leaders employ to address student, family, staff, or other stakeholder concerns. The role the participants play is very important because it can lead to ideas and strategies to address concerns such as chronic absenteeism, racial conflict, or mental health crises.

Audience – Stakeholders who would be vested in the success of collaborative partnerships such as a workshop or focus group include the students themselves, but also people outside of the school, such as employees within organizations (e.g., College Board), state and local professional organizations (e.g., National Association for College Admissions Counseling), and colleges and universities that can add valuable reciprocal opportunities for school counselor trainees, school counselor site supervisors, and schools where the services are being conducted and supervised.

Workshop sessions can be formal or impromptu. In other words, these sessions can be informational or simply a place to reflect and seek support from others with similar things to consider. Offering family support in the form of a workshop will entail the leaders differentiating the content to match both the variations of families who may or may not actively engage on their own. Take, for instance, discussion of details useful for transitioning from Kindergarten to first grade and all that is associated with this, or the major transition from collaborative reading that occurs up to second grade to reading independently, which is usually required during third grade. There are also some important transitions that happen when going from junior high to high school and beyond. College and career readiness can be helpful for families with youth who will soon make critical decisions. However, focus groups, whether formal or informal, are less likely to occur impromptu because there is a lot of planning, recruitment, and data analysis that will need to be considered before these groups are held.

Timeline – The different types of groups that are discussed in the activity above would have different timelines. For instance, a workshop might have a few planning sessions (e.g., goals, objectives, and curriculum development), a session or session(s) (e.g., an actual day or number of hours of meeting/work time over the course of several days), and some time for reflection and/or evaluation. The actual scheduling of these sessions will vary, but having a clear sense of the projected schedule ahead of time will help to give the participants an idea of the time commitment and the extent to which this matches their own. In addition to the projected scheduling of the group, session details such as start and ending times can also be predetermined based on the aims of the group. In the case of a focus group these sessions could last approximately 60 to 90 minutes, with the latter providing a good amount of time to develop group cohesion. That said, planning, recruitment, interview protocol development, data gathering, materials (e.g., video/audio recorders), data analysis, and reporting will need to be considered when creating a timeline for focus groups.

Expected outcomes – The goals and objectives at the onset for both the workshop and focus groups will help to drive the focus. The major outcomes targeted include delivering content or hearing the voices of more families to help foster environments of inclusion and to seek the expertise of stakeholders (e.g., families, students, staff or others) so they may be able to help out in significant ways. The participants leading a workshop or focus group will have expected outcomes, and the participants who are actually attending the workshop or offering feedback in a focus group will likely have outcomes that include utilizing the information discussed during the sessions or reflecting on ideas to further address the topic of inquiry. There will always be other benefits and challenges that arise during a workshop or focus group, especially when leaders and participants have the chance to use group experiences, interactions, and conflicts that arise in these groups.

Pulling It All Together

Collaboration invites dynamic interaction and engagement with two or more parties with a shared goal or task to work towards. For counselors and within the school setting, these collaborations occur on a daily basis and can involve any number of stakeholders, such as students, teachers, parents, administrators, families, and other school support personnel or staff. Group leadership skills provide a smooth transition for counselors, amplifying the importance of inclusion of all parties involved. This can be especially important when we consider situations that involve children and adolescents in a collaboration process with adults. Adults and school personnel have a responsibility to model healthy and adaptive communication, problem-solving, intentional listening (even when one may perceive a suggestion or comment to be unfavorable), mindfulness of cultural perspectives that may influence the process or outcomes, and citizenship. If the universal goals for PreK-12 schools include the creation of environments for students to thrive academically while learning and practicing soft skills and coping skills that will support transitions and contribute to their future success as citizens of the world later in life, adults modeling healthy behaviors during collaborations can be a profound teachable moment.

DISCUSSION QUESTIONS

1. Consider the information shared in this chapter on the work of Salvador Minunchin and Virginia Satir, two well-regarded pioneers who have contributed to the family therapy specialization. What tenets from their approaches align with practices you are already engaged in now? Are there tenets described that you could try to implement?

2. How might you assess your current communication style? What parts of your worldview and core value system may be covertly influencing how you communicate with others?

3. How might your communication style change when you are highly stressed? Excited and enthusiastic? Curious or brainstorming?

4. What might be some of the advantages and possible challenges for students as well as their families when they consider collaborations in the school setting? Consider the following scenario as a case discussion:

One of the families in your district is the Abara family, and they are on your caseload as the counselor at the middle school. Mr. Abara emigrated with his parents from Africa as a young child to the United States and grew up here, receiving citizenship years ago. His wife was born and raised in the United States, unclear and indifferent to know or learn about her genealogical background. They have three sons: Akito, who was adopted from Japan as a toddler and excelled academically such that he earned a full scholarship to Virginia Tech University; Zane, the Abara's first biological son, who barely passed high school last academic year and immediately enlisted in the military; and Joseph, who has been adopted officially by the Abaras but is actually Mrs. Abara's sister's child. They became guardians after a fatal accident took the lives of Joseph's parents. Joseph transferred to the district and moved in full time with the Abaras at the start of seventh grade. He is now in the eighth grade, where you are a counselor. Although Joseph has average academic performance, as indicated on his report cards, and seems, although quiet, to interact with his peers, he has recently shared with you that he isn't sure if "he's in the right body" and "feels uncomfortable" more often than not. In a recent conversation just with the parents, the father shared they are now expecting their fourth child in their family.

   a. What might be some of the assumptions, biases, prejudices, advantages, challenges, barriers, communication styles, and strategies for effective collaborations with the student (Joseph) still enrolled in the district and the family (Mrs. and Mr. Abara)? How might the responses modify if collaborations are with teachers? With administration?
   b. What supports might be most helpful to addressing Joseph's SEL needs based on the information presented? What additional information will be helpful to obtain to guide future steps?
   c. What supports might be most helpful to assisting the parents and family overall, based on the information presented? What additional information will be helpful to obtain to guide future steps?
   d. What additional continuing education or professional development may be helpful to you as a practicing school counselor to more effectively work with this student or family? What resources will be most helpful to you? How might you advocate within your school to obtain the continuing education or professional development you've identified using collaboration, adaptive communication, and group leadership skills?

REFERENCES

American School Counselors Association [ASCA] (2019). *The ASCA National model: A framework for school counseling programs* (4th ed.). Alexandria, VA: American School Counselors Association.

Baker, S. B., Robichaud, T. A., Dietrich, V. C. W., Wells, S. C., & Schreck, R. E. (2009). School counselor consultation: A pathway to advocacy, collaboration, and leadership. *Professional School Counseling, 12*(3), 200–206. https://doi.org/10.1177/2156759X0901200301

Brigman, G., Villares, E., & Webb, L. (2018). *Evidence-based school counseling: A student success approach.* Routledge.

Brothers, J. B. (Ed.). (2011). *Virginia Satir: Foundational ideas.* Routledge Taylor & Francis.

Bryan, J., & Henry, L. (2012). A model for building school–family–community partnerships: Principles and process. *Journal of Counseling & Development, 90*(4), 408–420. https://doi.org/10.1002/j.1556-6676.2012.00052.x

Cohen, J. (2006). Social, emotional, ethical, and academic education: Creating a climate for learning, participation in democracy, and well-being. *Harvard Educational Review, 76*(2), 201–237.

Cook, A. L., Troeger, R., Shah, A., Donahue, P., & Curley, M. (2020). Reenvisioning family–school–community partnerships: Reflecting on five years of dialogues on race programming within an urban school community. *School Community Journal, 30*(2), 121–154.

Darensbourg, A., Perez, E., & Blake, J. J. (2010). Overrepresentation of African American males in exclusionary discipline: The role of school-based mental health professionals in dismantling the school to prison pipeline. *Journal of African American Males in Education, 1,* 196–211.

Davidson, T. & Burson, K. (2017) Keep those kids out: Nativism and attitudes toward access to public education for the children of undocumented immigrants. *Journal of Latinos and Education, 16*(1), 41-50. https://doi: 10.1080/15348431.2016.1179189

Delgado, R., & Stefancic, J. (2001). *Critical Race Theory: An introduction.* NYU Press.

Devaney, E., & Berg, J. (2016). Creating healthy schools: Ten key ideas for the social and emotional learning and school climate community. *The 10.* Education Policy Center at American Institutes for Research. https://www.air.org/sites/default/files/downloads/report/Ten-Key-Ideas-for-Social-Emotional-Learning-School-Climate-Occtober-2016.pdf

Durlak, J. A., Weissberg, R. P., Dymnicki, A. B., Taylor, R. D., & Schellinger, K. (2011). The impact of enhancing students' social and emotional learning: A meta-analysis of school-based universal interventions. *Child Development, 82,* 405–432.

Greenberg, M. T., Domitrovich, C. E., Weissberg, R. P., & Durlak, J. A. (2017). Social and emotional learning as a public health approach to education. *Future of Children, 27*(1), 13–32.

Gregory, A., Skiba, R. J., & Noguera, P. A. (2010). The achievement gap and the discipline gap: Two sides of the same coin? *Educational Researcher, 39*(1), 59–68. https://doi.org/10.3102/0013189X09357621

Guth, L. J., Pollard, B. L., Nitza, A., Puig, A., Chan, C. D., Singh, A. A., & Bailey, H. (2019). Ten strategies to intentionally use group work to transform hate, facilitate courageous conversations, and enhance community building. *Journal for Specialists in Group Work, 44*(1), 3–24. https://doi.org/10.1080/01933922.2018.1561778

Kervick, C. T., Garnett, B., Moore, M., Ballysingh, T. A., & Smith, L. C. (2020). Introducing restorative practices in a diverse elementary school to build community and reduce exclusionary discipline: Year one processes, facilitators, and next steps. *School Community Journal, 30*(2), 155–184.

Lareau, A., & Horvat, E. M. (1999). Moments of social inclusion and exclusion race, class, and cultural capital in family-school relationships. *Sociology of Education, 72*(1), 37–53. https://doi.org/10.2307/2673185

Lorie, A., Reinero, D. A., Phillips, M., Zhang, L., & Riess, H. (2017). Culture and nonverbal expressions of empathy in clinical settings: A systemic review. *Patient Education and Counseling, 100*, 411-424. http://dx.doi.org/10.1016/j.pec.2016.09.018

McDonough, P. M. (2004). *The school-to-college transition: Challenges and prospects.* American Council on Education, Center for Policy Analysis.

McClafferty Jarsky, K., McDonough, P. M., & Núñez, A. M. (2009). Establishing a college culture in secondary schools through P-20 collaboration: A case study. Journal of *Hispanic Higher Education, 8*(4), 357–373.

Minunchin, S., & Fishman, H. C. (1981). *Family therapy techniques.* Harvard University Press.

Minunchin, S., Lee, W. Y., & Simon, G. M. (2006). *Mastering family therapy: Journeys of growth and transformation* (2nd ed.). John Wiley & Sons.

Singh, A. A., Nassar, S. C., Arredondo, P., & Toporek, R. (2020). The past guides the future: Implementing the multicultural and social justice counseling competencies. *Journal of Counseling and Development, 98*, 238-252.

Solorzano, D. G. (1998) Critical race theory, race and gender microaggressions, and the experience of Chicana and Chicano scholars, *International Journal of Qualitative Studies in Education, 11*(1), 121-136, DOI: 10.1080/095183998236926

Yosso, T. J., Smith, W. A., Ceja, M., & Solórzano, D. G. (2009). Critical Race Theory, racial microaggressions, and campus racial climate for Latina/o undergraduates. *Harvard Educational Review, 79*(4), 659–690.

7

21st-Century Education

Technology, Expansion of Virtual School Settings, and Societal Hot Topics

T echnology is changing the way in which we live in this society as well impacting our PreK-12 school environments. Americans, and others around the globe, experienced this directly and abruptly as a direct result of the COVID-19 global pandemic that interrupted the 2019–2020 academic year, catapulting schools to immerse themselves in technology to accomplish essential learning objectives. The aftermath of the abrupt shift continues to have a dramatic impact after a full year of implementation, with significant learning and modifications being identified to improve and enhance quality experiences for learners and educators. It is surmised that these results utilizing technology will stay with us as a newly defined part of the American educational system (and likely other countries as well) for many years that follow.

Many students, families, and educators are technologically savvy as a part of engaging and living their daily lives. Technology is a common and accessible platform that many individuals can use to access news, engage with family and friends, establish new connections, and experience the world through others' perspectives. We are mindful that although access to technology for a majority of Americans may appear to be an automatic assumption based on an acknowledgment of the United States offering many first-world privileges to its citizens, not all students, families, and educators may have access to technology or to equipment or services (e.g., Internet) that support the technological requirements to engage in virtual schooling. For example, many families across the country have one computer in the home that all family members share. When there are multiple children, this can become a barrier to access, because they cannot all use the same computer at the same time to engage in their studies. Another example may be a family that has more than one computer in the home, but the Internet service available in their geographic area or the service level the family can afford to subscribe to may have limited bandwidth for the amount of simultaneous activity required or may not have dependable connections. These differences outside of the school building have been magnified as a result of the global pandemic and the massive shift to virtual educational that occurred in the 2019–2020 and 2020–2021 academic years.

Several tools, applications (apps), software, and devices have been created to support the larger learning and development process in and outside of the school building. As a country and culture, most people are "connected 24/7" and may not recognize the degree of connection they may actually have to technology. Consider this—when there is an unexpected power outage with the electric company or the Internet goes down unexpectedly on any normal day, how do you react? What are your first thoughts? Behaviors? Feelings? For many, it may mean a speedy transition into a high-stress, frustrated, or even crisis mode. How often do you respond calmly, recognizing that it is a situation out of your control and that it will soon be fixed? How often do you smile at the unexpected opportunity you have been given to "disconnect" and focus on another work-related task that does not include technology? Do you take the opportunity to step outside for fresh air and sunshine or a brief play session with the family dog or cat? American culture relies heavily on technology, and has become comfortable with a fast-paced, technology-dependent perspective in many situations. Even while sleeping, many people have a smartwatch or fitness tracker monitoring their heart rate or other biometric data connected to a smartphone or cloud service. As we focus our scope on how technology is informing and affecting not only American culture, but specifically the culture of learning within education, including experiences and opportunities for students and teachers, it is imperative that educators become well adept and equipped to meet these changing and growing modifications. Integrating group leadership skills to engage within the school building as well as support the students, families, and broader school communities recognizing differences with technology is paramount so as not to create additional barriers and divisions.

Foundational Knowledge, Contextual Dimensions, and Practice

Technology can be used to enhance group work delivered in school settings to meet the needs effectively, efficiently, and inclusively of its community members. There are also several cautions that are unique to integrating technology as an intentional and predominant tool as we consider the public PreK-12 school setting. This chapter will discuss foundational elements to the virtual school environment that has surged in popularity and need as a result of the global pandemic. We will also identify strategies for successful integration of technology as we highlight the increased access to education across diverse communities, students, and families that is often noted as the largest benefit to virtual school platforms as well as highlight areas of notable caution or possible barriers to the process so that prevention efforts may be taken. We recognize that the evolution and development of technology changes at an unprecedented rate in this 21st century. As such, our suggestions for best practice are grounded more in the processes and behavioral actions a counselor or group leader may consider to prepare and facilitate their group. It is less about the specific vendor who supplies the technology (although still vet vendors!) and more about the technology and the process of how it is used. This perspective, we hope, will make the content offered in this chapter more transferable and able to stand the test of time while the specific vendors, technology platforms, and tools continue their rapid evolution. The objectives for this chapter are as follows:

1. Define *communication* in a virtual world versus a traditional face-to-face world, and explain why open, transparent, and timely communication is essential.

2. Describe virtual schools.

3. Explore and understand the growing digital barrier.

4. Identify best practice considerations for navigating the three essential environments.

Communication Is Key

Although it may seem obvious in a counseling-focused book, it is important to reiterate how essential communication is to the overall process, productivity, and potential for groups and its members to achieve meaning. At its basic form, communication is an exchange of information (verbally and/ or nonverbally) from one individual to another or more delivered by an identified mechanism or process. Communication may be delivered through written words (e.g., newspapers, articles, blog posts, books), verbal words (e.g., radio, television news, video clips on streaming Internet platforms, conversations between one or more people "live" and synchronously), and nonverbal messages (e.g., body language, voice intonation and inflection; interpretations of additional meanings verbal words chosen may have).

Communication also serves as the bedrock to identifying and illuminating intentional and unintentional messages and meaning. This is where ambiguity, perspectives, and filters (known and unknown) to the communicators may influence the information being transmitted and how it is ultimately received. Consider your own experiences where you have received an email or a text message or have read a social media post and needed to pause to consider "Wait?! Is that really what they meant to say?" Or you reply back only to receive a response that indicates there had been a misunderstanding.

In group settings, this becomes even more complex because the influences are not solely between the two parties that are communicating. The receiver is also influenced by external messages and information that are being subtly and directly transmitted to them while the direct messenger is actively communicating. Considering a clear example with students in a school setting, when two students are communicating in a group situation or a student and teacher are communicating, all others in the room (or the "group") are watching the exchange as observers, and the communicators are typically directly aware of this. The messages (verbal and nonverbal) that are also being received by the "observers" who are playing a direct role in the communicating may have a profound influence on how those communicating are receiving and interpreting messages based on their own filters, perspectives, and any additional ambiguity that may be present in the direct communication itself. From this lens, we can see how group communication is more about the *process*. True, the outcome-driven event or function is still a very important element, but it is the process that makes the outcome possible. Communication helps to facilitate many of the other goals and aspects of healthy and cohesive group experiences, such as building interpersonal relationships, trust, and rapport among the group members.

Schools often represent many of the diverse elements within the nearby communities. Counselors and others leading groups are encouraged to pay close attention to communication in all modalities as a way of supporting a school culture and community of culturally respectful and civic-minded growth for all. "Humor" or "teasing" often is observed between and among students. This can be a common form of communication used to establish in-group and out-group membership at the student/peer level. Racism, ethnic differences, and language, social, cognitive, or developmental delays are all examples of the root of the "humor" or "teasing" that may be evidenced. Due to technology, this maladaptive and damaging type of communication appears to be taking place more often on social media websites. These one-directional globally public forums invite a disillusioned understanding of the impact and affect words can have on others. This is an essential learning skill, yet without the immediate accountability and responsibility one will have for words communicated "in real time" with another or in a group, many individuals (students and adults) receive messages that their behavior and choice is without grave impact. These behaviors are evidenced in schools throughout the world and aided in speed and access through social media and electronic platforms.

These communication habits often serve as powerful building blocks that do not have far to grow to become problematic bullying behaviors. They are impacting all building levels, from elementary through high school. It is incumbent upon every member of the school system to take intentional steps to stop and change these behaviors and their tragic outcomes. Although not all situations may be fatal, the damaging effect on intra- and interpersonal development can still be profound. The following are merely a few examples of the catastrophic and fatal effect that maladaptive communication can have:

- In 2006, a 13-year-old in Missouri, Megan Meier, killed herself after the mother of a former friend created a fictitious profile online to harass her.
- In 2009, an 11-year-old in Springfield, Massachusetts, Carl Joseph Walker-Hoover, hung himself with an extension cord due to being bullied and repeatedly called "gay."
- In 2010, a 15-year old, Phoebe Prince, was bullied by students from her school (in-person and via online modes). She ended her life by hanging herself in her home. She was bullied, in part, due to her accent, because she and her family had recently immigrated to the United States from a small village in Ireland.
- In 2017 in Cincinnati, Ohio, 8-year-old Gabriel Taye was physically accosted in a school bathroom. The students who were the perpetrators continued beating Gabriel for nearly 5 minutes after Gabriel appeared to have been beaten unconscious, which was noted as part of the assault was captured on surveillance video. Two days later, Gabriel's mother found him dead next to his bed at home.

As we consider how communication may be similar and different when carried out in a traditional face-to-face modality versus being in an electronic/virtual modality, we easily see where more and more variables to confound communication rise to the surface. Engaging and intentionally supporting open, transparent, and timely communication helps to mitigate the confounding variables that add to the innate complexities within communication. Helping to educate and inform children and adolescents to learn *why* this is important versus simply expecting the behavior can be a helpful approach. Repeatedly engaging in conversations, even if they are uncomfortable, to explore and discuss different perspectives, attempting to balance situations that require discipline and situations that may be aided through a "teachable moment," can influence a culture or system.

As we continue in this digital age, groups are increasing their utilization of technology and/ or holding groups via virtual platforms with more frequency. A recent surge in these trends may be attributed to the COVID-19 pandemic. However, even before the pandemic, many industries were increasing their use of technology. We observed this with the rise of virtual schooling options among public charter schools and for-profit organizational schools at the PreK-12 level. Regardless of whether the intended group is a part of a virtual school setting working with children and adolescents or a group serving an adult population, there are several technology and online norms, behaviors, and strategies that may assist with overall engagement and reaching effective outcomes. For example, it will likely be the need that increased and perhaps more structured communication will be required to maintain similar levels that would have been observed if communication were occurring in a traditional face-to-face environment. As we begin to substitute or eliminate pathways for engaging in the complexity that is communication, we add additional room for misinterpretation and ambiguity. To counterbalance this, increased efforts and structure often help.

Understanding Virtual School

Homeschooling and virtual schooling have been available educational options in the United States for decades, long before the COVID-19 pandemic swept the country. However, many students and families may not have been aware of these options because the traditional brick-and-mortar, face-to-face schooling option has been readily available and accessible.

For families who select homeschooling, regardless of the varying requirements noted between states, the parents intentionally "sign up" to be the educator of record and have the autonomy to create a "school day" and "school week" structure that fits best within their family and home to fulfill state-mandated requirements.

Virtual schools started establishing roots within the U.S. education system in the mid-1990s following the growth and expansion of the Internet (Barbour & Reeves, 2009). This is not surprising given the generally accepted definition of *virtual schools* is a school (or organization) that has approval to educate and operate as an approved school by a state or related governing body with jurisdiction associated with the American educational system. Typically, these schools are known for offering most, if not all, coursework and requirements using a distance-delivery method that may be either independent, synchronous, or asynchronous.

Some local school districts have offered and managed their own virtual schooling options, often with lower enrollment numbers and with specific eligibility criteria to manage the limited resources available. Data gathered from the 2015–2016 and 2016–2017 school years show that large virtual schools operated by for-profit education management organizations (EMOs) enrolled an average of 1,288 students, nearly three times the number of students as compared to nonprofit EMOs and independent virtual schools that are not affiliated with an EMO. These data also illustrate that, relative to national public school enrollment, virtual schools had substantially fewer minority students, fewer low-income students, and very few English language learners (ELLs) compared to the national averages. While the student–teacher ratio for brick-and-mortar schools nationally is 16:1, the student–teacher ratio for virtual schools could be two to three times higher. However, because many states do not have the infrastructure, policies, or legislation in place requiring the same school data and accountability as brick-and-mortar schools, the data on virtual schools are limited. The data that are available show that virtual schools underperform academically. As we consider the nearly triple class size and the likelihood that a teacher would not have any or very limited professional and clinical training to be a teacher in a virtual school, it is not shocking to see poor student performance data. The American education system was not designed for virtual schools, and it has not provided resources, training, or transitional support to students or educators. And, this was all before the global pandemic that forced schools and districts across the nation to transition to a virtual platform to meet COVID-19 safety guidelines (Miron et al., 2018).

Training programs at the undergraduate and graduate level leading to a license as an educator in the American educational system does not require any coursework or clinical supervised experience training specific to virtual education or the virtual school environment. Training programs and federal, state, and university requirements are designed based on a brick-and-mortar educational system. Even some of the more recent online universities that are approved to offer degree and licensing-only programs for education are still focused on a model that trains teachers for the brick-and-mortar school setting even if their experience as a teacher/educator candidate in training was completed in a hybrid or 100% online virtual university classroom setting. It is likely that in the coming years training curriculums will begin to expand in order to address online learning and development and related skills courses will be added to program and licensure requirements to support the digital learning age that we are now all a part of. In the meantime, there is still an imbalance between the perception and deployment of brick-and-mortar schools and virtual schools. Unfortunately, this is not a "copy/paste" scenario, as was illustrated in the wake of the global pandemic when districts across all grade levels (including universities) scrambled to shift to a fully online delivery service in the midst of the 2020–2021 academic year.

Although many systems, states, and federal government stakeholders extended tremendous leniency for students and districts, many waiving student performance, testing, and accountability requirements for the last quarter of the 2020–2021 academic year, the crippling effects from the global pandemic knocked the American education system even further behind. Leading into the 2021–2022 academic year, many students, parents, teachers, counselors, school administrators, and overall states are dramatically behind in reaching desired and set learning goals. Consistent with data gleaned to illustrate student performance from virtual schools gathered as recently as 5 years ago, students are falling behind in academic growth and development (Miron et al., 2018). For many students, lack of structure, lack of direct support from a teacher, lack of indirect support from students or support personnel in the school building, and the ambiguity from being at home while also "in school" are contributing factors. When we dive even deeper and explore patterns that are becoming barriers for student success in the virtual school setting, we also find that the individual development of the child influences their engagement, and thus performance in the virtual school environment. Overall, as part of larger cultural and societal trends observed independent of the education system, we have observed American culture drifting away from individual and family values, work ethics, and societal/civic norms that may be advantageous to students given the current landscape of the world.

Many values, ethics, and practical norms are transferable to the brick-and-mortar experience, and also serve as characteristics and traits commonly recognized as essential for 21st-century adulthood and the workforce. Characteristics and traits that can be overtly observed to positively influence preparedness and performance within the new PreK-12 "virtual school day" include, but are not limited to, grit; autonomous learning; intrinsic motivation; perseverance; humility; a thirst for knowledge; interpersonal communication and relationships to share knowledge and learn from others; inquisitive collaborative communities; courage to take risks and learn from mistakes, setbacks, or failures; self-efficacy, self-concept, and self-esteem; short-term and long-term goal setting; positivity in the face of challenges; creative and flexible thinking; higher-level critical thinking; and self-discipline.

Exploring and Understanding the Growing Digital Barrier

Just as there are covert barriers that may serve as risk factors for individuals at different stages of development, there are barriers that may hinder the growth and development of an individual in the digital age. Often, these *digital barriers* serve to hinder access and/or equality in a virtual environment for one or more individuals. Our creation of this new term *digital barrier* seeks to operationalize and offer a definition that stretches beyond being a novice at using technology or a specific learning management system. It seeks to expand beyond a lack of exposure to an individual's understanding of how to use technology and speaks of the ways technology may create barriers that inhibit growth, communication, collaborations, or interpersonal relationships.

Independent of country or system, *quality education* is commonly understood to ensure inclusive and equitable access to learning and educational resources or supports as well as to promote lifelong learning opportunities for all (Burbules et al., 2020). Impacts from a quality education contribute to a solid foundation of skills, knowledge, and growth opportunities for intra- and interpersonal development across the lifespan for any individual. Even depicted as the basis of several popular movies, a quality education can transform the lives of students as well as ripple into positive outcomes for the families they are a part of. Jain (2020) stated in a recent UNESCO report based on the effects of the COVID-19 pandemic that approximately 72% of academic institutions across the world closed or no longer supported traditional delivery of educational services. As the world and each country works to rebuild their infrastructures across all disciplines, educational systems are at the forefront. It is acknowledged that the impacts not only severely affect learning and student performance data on content knowledge acquisition, as demonstrated on high-stakes testing, but there have also been profound barriers for many students and families that extend beyond academic learning as a result of the school closures and shifts to virtual schooling (where available). Examples have included limited or no access to technology in the home for some families; disrupted meal service access for students; increased potential for physical effects from engaging in a digital environment at high frequencies daily; inconsistencies defining the "time on learning" when at home; possible increases in financial constraints for families; and a change in peer/social interactions that directly influence and inform child and adolescent development.

Limited or No Access to Technology in the Home

Not all individuals and families have computers, laptops, or devices at home, and not all have access to the Internet. Even if a family did have the equipment and Internet at their home, many families experienced inequities with the need and bandwidth. Both children and parents were now "schooling/working from home" simultaneously, meaning that if a family only had one computer in the house, splitting time between the adult and children for their respective needs was required. Additionally, those who had Internet service may or may not have had enough bandwidth to support the number of devices or the scope of work required at one time given the usage dramatically increased with the family all being at home.

Disrupted Meal Service Access

Countless students and families throughout the country depend on the meal services provided by the schools during and sometimes after school. With the closure of schools, for a brief period of time, schools were unable to offer any supplemental services for meals to students and their families. Many schools creatively identified solutions for outdoor pick up services only, but there were still very limited and slowly delivered opportunities at the beginning. Nearly a year after the onset of the pandemic crippling the American educational system, it is unclear if all meal service needs have been restored or are actively being addressed now for the number of families who are depending on this essential service from the PreK-12 schools.

Growing Physical Barriers in a High-Demand Digital Environment

Barriers may also stem from overuse of technology. A new societal norm emerged in 2020, with the term *zoom fatigue* capturing the overall mental, emotional, and physical exhaustion that one may experience when they find themselves continuously shifting from one Zoom meeting to the next, often with a break of less than 5 minutes between meetings, if a break was even obtainable between meetings. This fatigue has similar representation to behaviors and signs seen in burnout, but it is a different type of fatigue because the stimulus and the context for the ongoing stimulus are notably different. Overall wellness, balance, and self-care strategies are even more important now than before as one intentional and purposeful way to combat fatigue from overuse and requirement of being on a computer. The positive impacts will not only aid overall mental acuity, focus, and perseverance, but may also aid in physical systems such as decrease in ocular, neck, back, leg, and other muscular-skeletal discomfort or strain from stationary positioning for extended hours and staring at a computer screen that may also be in a room with less than ideal lighting for overall eye health.

Inconsistent "Time on School" for Learning and Academic Development

In the wake of the pandemic, many parents were forced into the temporary role of being an at-home teacher, regardless of whether it was related or of interest to their career. In addition to navigating and managing tumultuous waters within their own career, if they did not experience layoffs as a direct result of the pandemic, parents were also expected to immediately create the at-home space and support the continued learning of their children. These transitions between the traditional, hybrid, and virtual school settings have been very messy and inconsistent. It has given rise to frustration and human and technical barriers that may have gone unnoticed prior to the pandemic. Additional school supplies, tools for learning, or resources may have been unavailable or hard to come by. This is assuming that the financial health of the family permitted these additional unexpected expenses as well.

Limited or Delayed Social Development and Peer Interactions

Early pandemic safety guidelines required a minimum of 6 feet between people, as well as several months of stay-at-home pseudo-quarantine practices. This had a negative impact on the overall social-emotional development of children, given that we know that interaction with peers and friends, along with family, is critical at this developmental stage. Dating back to the 1800s, psychologists noted the influential experiences on individual identity and personality development observed in children and young adolescents with their peer group. Restricted to being with families as a result of the pandemic has limited or significantly reduced the amount of social contact and intra- as well as interpersonal development for many children.

Changes in Learning with Digital Technologies

Even before the global pandemic, the influence of digital technologies and learning management systems (LMS) in education from elementary through colleges and universities has been notable. Burbules et al. (2020) note some of the direct changes that can be seen within (1) our educational aims and objectives, (2) educational ecologies and contexts of learning, (3) the processes of learning, (4) the processes of teaching, and (5) educational governance and policy. As we have discussed earlier, these changes require us to reconsider and modify how we think, act, and evaluate our ways within the traditional (brick-and-mortar) educational system.

Entering the 21st century, we saw a rise in occupations and careers within the technology sector. Fields and industries that may not have been utilizing technology as directly or profoundly were adapting to changing needs and times to innovate, increase production, or meet other goals. Simultaneously, a rise in the need for "soft skills" was also regularly called for in the labor market. Interestingly, although technology appears to provide a disconnect and methodical, almost flat, affect connection, the labor market has been calling for an increase in workers with stronger interpersonal, communication, listening, critical-thinking, and adaptable creative skills. Regardless of the field or discipline, the assumption is that students who graduate from high school will have the transferable skills and knowledge base to engage in complex, higher-level critical thinking skills and capabilities in their postsecondary environments regardless of whether they choose to continue to the college/university setting, join the labor market, focus on family, or join the military. They will be citizens of the world.

In 2012 the National Education Association advocated for students learning and demonstrating skills as well as knowledge comprising the "four Cs": critical thinking, creativity, communication, and collaboration (Burbules et al., 2020). These areas include a focus on protective factors to positively inform development for the individual as well as support interpersonal relationships. The four Cs consist of skills and dispositions that influence school, work, and overall life, inviting flexible capabilities related to learning and supporting an individual's intrinsic capabilities to adapt to changing demands, rather than narrowly relying on specific subject-matter knowledge. There is transferability to the digital arena as well for learning and the workforce when we consider the four Cs. Burbules et al. (2020) identified the main areas illustrating the impact on digital learning to include: (1) the increasing need to critically assess the credibility of information accessed online; (2) interaction with a range of media and forms of expression, which digital natives both consume and create; (3) engaging with new forms of communication adapted to different kind of platforms, which suggest new models of literacy and fluency; and (4) social media and other applications that emphasize sharing and different forms of collaboration.

As we connect these concepts to the foundational tenets of group work and group counseling, we can see where there is natural overlap. Opportunities and value for communication, intra- and interpersonal growth and development, inviting creative and critical thinking to consider perspectives, situations, and feedback to explore meaning and future changes or behaviors. As a group leader, it is imperative to enter into the role and responsibility of leading a group with a purpose in mind. Have a framework for intentional practice that can support and guide you and the group process in efficient and effective ways. We offer one such framework in this book for your consideration, TRATE My Group, recognizing that there is no one way to be an effective group leader. However, note that there are many ways to hinder, stall, disrupt, or create barriers to group process, effectiveness, equitability, and overall success. Leaders without frameworks, without intentionality, without a mindful practice knowledgeable of the subject area as well as group process will more often than not prevent groups from being effective, efficient, and ultimately successful. Draw on the knowledge and skill base you have and seek to use group work in an intentional way to inform mindful practice that invites inclusion, respect, and diversity.

STOP AND REFLECT

Brief Self-Assessment of Overall Awareness

Linking to the four Cs of critical thinking, creativity, communication, and collaboration discussed above, reflect and note on the following.

TOPIC: _____

When you are engaged in the topic listed above, what percentage distribution is reflected with the four Cs?

- Critical thinking = _____ %
- Creativity = _____ %
- Communication = _____ %
- Collaboration = _____ %

TOTAL = 100%

Reflect on how you typically feel when you are engaged in this topic. Circle all that apply and add new feelings, as appropriate.

Tired	Sad	Excited	Anxious	Drained	Happy	Energetic
Calm	Disconnected	Innovative	Valued		Needed	Confused
Overwhelmed		Devalued		Empowered		Helpful

What are the primary thoughts or messages that typically repeat in your head when you are engaged in this topic?

Message/Thought 1: _____

Message/Thought 2: _____

Considering all of the information you've identified on this topic, what is one goal that you can achieve/accomplish within the next 2 weeks that will support you to be successful in this topic (no matter how big or small it might seem)? What is one goal that will build from the 2-week accomplishment that can be reasonably completed 1 month from today? What is one goal that will build from the 1-month success and continue the growth and success you are reaching within 3 months from today?

Today's date: _____

2 weeks from today will be (enter date): _____

2-week goal: _____

1 month from today will be (enter date): _____

1-month goal: _____

3 months from today will be (enter date): _____

3-month goal: _____

Brief Self-Assessment of Physical Status and Awareness

- For 1 week, keep track of what time you go to bed and what time you wake up. When you wake up, guess how long it may have taken for you to fall asleep. If you have a heart rate monitor (e.g., Fitbit, Apple watch, Whoop, etc.), you may have some of this data.

- Monitor your heart rate. Select five different times during the day when you will check your heart rate and blood pressure at the same time for 1 week. Look for patterns after you've gathered your data. Note any contextual factors that may be influencing your readings when you take your measurements.

- How hydrated are you? Most individuals are in a perpetual state of dehydration throughout the majority of their lives. Americans have access to water, yet many are not consuming even one-quarter of what they need to be for their bodies to be operating at full capacity. And, many make the process even harder by overconsuming caffeine daily and not nourishing themselves with a healthy diet and exercise. Log in ounces how much water you consume each day for 1 week. Remember, this is about awareness, not judgement.

- Are you eating enough, and enough "brain food" in particular? Keep a food journal/log for 1 week. This is not about counting calories or macronutrients; rather it is to help bring concrete data to the forefront to observe when you are eating, what you are eating, and how these pieces may be translating into helping or hindering a work environment that requires virtual presence.

Best Practice Considerations for Navigating the Three Essential Environments

It is important to consider how best practices will inform three essential environments that are fluidly operating now within and among most education (and noneducation) systems in the post-pandemic era. The three essential environments are: (1) traditional (i.e., face-to-face); (2) virtual, which is the equivalent of being 100% online or remote; and (3) hybrid, which splits time between face-to-face and virtual either on a daily or a weekly basis. Central factors that will influence all three environments for students, teachers, administrators, counselors, and families include access, digital literacy, imbalance or digital fatigue due to transitioning environments or a lack of clear structured boundaries to support consistent performance, and opportunities for interactive engagement between and among peers/members or the student/member and teacher/counselor/group leader. School counselors may also play a vital role as a support during times of transition between any of these essential environments for students, parents, and/or adults in the school building.

As a culture, a country, and an education system, we have rapidly redefined what technology means, needs, and how it is valued within the PreK-12 public schools (and in higher education or the workforce). In direct result of the COVID-19 pandemic, communities across America and the world saw an increase in virtual school formats across all education sectors, including public, private, charters, labs, and for profits. Taking mindful and intentional steps to create an online environment that is inclusive, engaging, and focused on learning, growth, and development can support meeting academic goals as well as minimize fatigue and stress that may be inherent in the transitions between traditional and virtual school environments. While the media may change, it is still critical to consider that the intersectionality of diversity and education have profound impacts and influences on children, adolescents, and adult development, including intra- and interpersonal relationships. A virtual school environment does not minimize, dismiss, or negate challenges that an individual may experience (before or after a transition to/from a virtual environment) around matters of identity, self-esteem/self-worth, race, gender, sexuality, or any other elements that contribute to the makeup of each unique person.

School counselors are often the only licensed and clinically trained support personnel to support prevention and intervention efforts advocating for community awareness as well as identification of barriers and adaptive growth strategies or interventions to assist with coping and behavior modifications that may be needed within a school environment. Depending on the topic area, school counselors often engage their myriad of skills to collaborate actively with external support resources for the student or the family, such as medical doctors, local law enforcement, external clinical therapists, or behavior specialists. These examples have been on the rise, especially in the last decade, paralleling the rise of mental health issues evidenced among children and adolescents around topics such as, but not limited to, bullying, substance or alcohol abuse, and suicidal ideation. Similar resources and skills may be needed regardless of the traditional in-person or virtual school environment. Focus on awareness/identification of barriers, adaptive strategies to cope, adapt, and overcome as well as advocacy. Although technology may provide opportunities for increased access or a perception of increased connection or accessibility, our goal at the root is still to create and foster healthy human connections for intra- and interpersonal adaptive growth and development.

In the traditional face-to-face environments, technology may be used to support or assist identified goals or processes, but it is rarely the prominent resource. Utilizing skills and concepts discussed earlier in this book such as communication, listening, and various group norms can all be thoughtfully engaged with more focus than technology. These efforts enhance the overall intra- and interpersonal experiences. However, when we are in a hybrid or a 100% virtual modality, what are essential areas to be mindful of as we strive for continued effective and efficient best practices in our work?

Applications within the virtual environment (hybrid or fully remote) are often regarded as an equalizer inviting access to diverse groups of people who may not otherwise be able to participate or consider opportunities. Although this may be true for some variables that may be prohibitive to access, such as geographic barriers, it may also be trading one set of challenges for another. And while geographic "walls" come down, new variables such as (1) fiscal access to obtain the technological equipment required to engage in a virtual school, (2) paying monthly Internet bills to local providers that offer a bandwidth strong enough to operate the various technology platforms and tools required in the virtual school, and (3) a level of digital or technological literacy to operate and navigate the equipment, software, and expectations in what is often a more autonomous setting are three general examples of essential daily requirements for success.

Although the modern convenience of technology is helpful for some students or adults, engaging in a virtual school or working environment serves to enhance blurred boundaries and invites "strangers" into a personal space, usually within one's home. Geographical and logistical boundaries, even though they may have been figurative, provided clear separation between the roles any individual has in different parts of their lives. When they are in a school building, they are a "student" or "teacher" or "counselor." When they are in their home, they are a "child" or "brother/sister" or "parent" or "spouse/ partner." When they are at the local coffee shop or restaurant with their friends, the role changes still. This is not to say that the person's identity changes, but the relationships, expectations, behavioral norms, and customs of the self and others within that environment were established. In the new virtual world, for many, these boundaries are now ambiguous or nearly nonexistent. For some with limited space at home or limited space that offers no distraction, they may need to be in a bedroom or a room used for other purposes. This creates a pseudo-voyeuristic element that is often not addressed but influences the perceptions and interpretations people may have about an individual regardless of whether they are actively or verbally contributing to a virtual environment. Compartmentalizing and disentangling identities and roles has become harder in these post-pandemic time. It is important to acknowledge how personal and professional spaces are commingled. Some people make judgments, or can be uncomfortable seeing themselves in a mirror so when they see their presentation of the camera, that can send different messages—assumptions of not wanting to connect or of not wanting to be seen that day. Engaging skills and training counselors have around group dialogue, counselors are encouraged to process and address early on assumptions and norms that might influence the overall group process; for example, addressing interpretations people may make regarding backgrounds, extraneous noises, observations of the ways they engage with family members, or a perceived lack of engagement if a mute button is on or a camera is off during a synchronous session. One example of how to create a similar environment in a virtual setting is to ask all members of the group to use the same background or wallpaper during synchronous sessions. This is similar to all members being physically in the same room. This small update to the background may reduce or altogether eliminate one possible area of distraction from engagement in the group process.

Whether the application for the virtual environment is meeting the needs of students or adults, having an intentional framework to plan and prepare will aid everyone in the process. Task, psycho-educational, and even counseling group types are all realistic and available options for facilitating in the virtual PreK-12 school environment. Strategies for preparation and facilitation may be modified to more directly account for the shift in needs and variables that are inherent in changing the setting, as illustrated above.

Practical Suggestions for Group Leaders/Facilitators

For all three types of groups that might be used in a PreK-12 school environment, a group leader/facilitator may find it helpful to integrate free software and tools that are commonly used for active engagement. When using new tools it is important to consider how the tool directly connects to the content or learning outcomes that are anticipated for that session/day/activity before deploying them. There still needs to be an intentional purpose when integrating tools, even if they are only used for a few seconds to invite a new visual or creative stimulus to jolt the brain. Most children in elementary and middle school levels have an attention span of approximately 8 to 10 minutes. Most adults have an attention span of 13 to 20 minutes, depending upon the content. This assumes that consistent attention is given to one format or type of stimulus (e.g., lecturing/speaking, watching a video clip, reading, etc.). Engaging, short activities that are directly connected to the content being discussed can have an overall positive impact on attention, retention, engagement, and dynamic learning, which are all noted to have direct impacts on academic achievement and student performance. Examples of such activities include the following:

- *Brief quizzes or polls.* Quizzes and polls invite semi-structured or structured feedback, reactions, or insights and can be used to quickly assess learning. They can be useful in transitioning between virtual, hybrid, and traditional settings. Many tools today include both a website and a mobile app version. Free tools that may be considered include, but are not limited to, Kahoot, PollEverywhere, Slido, and Word Cloud.
- *Video or audio clips.* Multimedia clips can may be created from external sources or prerecorded by the instructor/leader or a member of that school community or another person whose perspective or role may connect with the audience being served. These may be housed on free platforms such as YouTube, Knowmia, Panopto, or Google Drive or another cloud-based storage area.
- *Interactive discussion boards.* Discussion boards can be used to continue conversations in synchronous or asynchronous delivery modes. It will be helpful for the leader/facilitator to illustrate or provide explicit guidelines as to the length and expectations of the content before the members begin using the platform. Clarifying these expectations transparently and universally in advance helps to invite all members in an inclusive manner while also keeping the goal of the activity manageable and time-limited. A recommendation for middle school age is to focus on two to three sentences. For high school and older, it is reasonable

to recommend one to two paragraphs as the expectation. Free tools that can invite this type of dynamic interaction among the members and the leader might include a discussion board embedded with the learning management system (LMS) that a school owns a subscription service to (e.g., Blackboard, Moodle, Desire2Learn, CANVAS); JamBoard as an add-on to the Google Suite; or Google Docs that share collaborative editing access.

As technology is integrated, even if only for a brief period of time, group leaders/facilitators are cautioned to be vigilant for warning signs that could be indicators of problematic behaviors. This may be informed by ambiguity with transferring habits or behaviors that may have already been learned as acceptable in other arenas of the child's life but do not sustain in an educational environment. As discussed above, communication styles and interpretations may be more susceptible in a virtual setting given there are significantly limited ways of transmitting information. When in person, we can communicate by taking in and interpreting verbal information as well as nonverbal information such as body language, tone of speech and intonation, inflections, and different physical gestures used to supplement the information being shared. If we are in a conversation with more than one person, we also have additional information gleaned from observing the reactions and considering direct verbal contributions by others as well as the primary communicator. In a virtual environment, especially depending on the number of participants, this may not be a possibility. With many video-conferencing software platforms (e.g., Zoom, WebEx, Google Classroom), synchronous meetings are often limited to 16 people being viewed on the screen at one time, presuming the individual has their account set up in a gallery setting to look at the cameras of others. This number decreases when the screen is needed for viewing documents related to the discussion. Thus, communication may often be relying only on verbal (nonvisual) contributions, similar to being on a telephone call with more than one party on the line. Caution areas to note are often based in misunderstandings or misinterpretations that may derive from the context offered or assumptions or judgments made (consciously or subconsciously) about nonverbal elements, including, but not limited to, if a person is muted or not using a camera influencing perceptions of interest or engagement (especially if this is not normed at the beginning to reduce feedback); what type of background a person may have, whether Zoom wallpaper or an area in their home; the number of disruptions the person might have from children or animals, and how they respond to the disruptions in the middle of a meeting/conversation; or whether people contribute verbally or not. One way to circumvent this if it occurs is to address it in a respectful manner that invites a "teachable moment" and allows an intentional discussion of netiquette, roles, and expectations of all members while in the virtual space.

The size of a virtual group is critical and often requires modification of what would be appropriate or conducive in a traditional in-person format. For example, in virtual school environments within the college/university setting, many graduate-level content classes (not clinical supervised internship) in the counseling training area have a capacity of enrollment of 20 or 24 students. While this has been a general norm among counseling training programs nationwide for years in a traditional setting, there can be severe limitations and barriers to reaching similar levels of dynamic engagement, achieving similar learning outcomes for all students, and being able to provide the depth of integrated learning for each student appropriate to their developmental level as a counselor-in-training when the class environment switches to the virtual environment. For this reason, it is not uncommon to see some graduate programs decrease the enrollment capacity for 100% online counselor training courses, when possible. Alternatively, if the enrollment capacity cannot be reduced, instructors can employ creative teaching strategies to blend asynchronous and synchronous delivery modes to meet learning outcomes, but modifying the synchronous time to groups with an average size of eight students to one instructor (note the parallel here with the recommended group size!).

Related, the time expected to actively engage in a traditional in-person group format could easily be 90 to 110 minutes. However, in a fully virtual environment, it is often very difficult to engage in a group format for more than 1 hour, and this assumes that the members are adults. This time for active engagement decreases even further with younger people. Group leaders are encouraged to consider creative strategies to blend physical engagement, when possible, with the need to be in the virtual space. For example, when a question is posed by a group leader inviting members to reflect, instead of having everyone remain seated as they consider the prompt, a group leader may choose to invite members to stand up and stretch or walk around in the room where they are located while still on camera so they know the members have not left the room. This invitation provides a blend of the physical stimulus while still engaged in the activity needed and is likely to positively influence active engagement.

Fluidity of conversation and dialogue between and among members and leaders as well as the opportunities to process nonverbal behaviors or communication is incredibly challenging in a virtual environment. When in a traditional in-person setting, it is common for groups to be physically organized to take a circle shape. This structure naturally invites fluidity in communication and fosters connections. It supports group leaders operating in the "here and now" to best balance the needs of the group as well as the larger group goals and objectives. However, when in a virtual setting, barriers may exist that inhibit the open and fluid exchanges between members and/or leaders. Common examples may include barriers with camera functionality or quality, speaker/microphone functionality or quality, mitigating background noises when trying to speak so as not to add additional distractions, and body language that may be consciously or unconsciously influenced by other environmental factors that no one else in the group can see or have awareness of. In virtual meetings, body language may send different messages, and thus influence insights or interpretations by others. This is an area of caution for group leaders and may be helped by addressing this as a possibility in the first group meeting/session to clarify how it can be appropriately identified and addressed if someone in the group experiences this. One example may be if one member in the virtual meeting is viewed by others as sitting with their arms crossed and leaning back in a chair. Typically, these nonverbal behaviors may be interpreted by other members in the group as a sign of that person being disconnected, disengaged, or excluding themselves from the group conversation. In person, leaders and members can observe this and address it both with verbal and nonverbal dialogue in a timely manner, acting in the "here and now." In the virtual setting, the slower pace and processes of dialogue may hinder this being replicated, and thus perceptions or observations may continue going unaddressed for longer than they would otherwise have, or may not be easily observed by all depending on how many were a part of the virtual session and the other screen requirements that were needed. Group leaders in a virtual setting may often need to have their screen on a "share mode." meaning they may not see the gallery of the thumbnails of members on the group and may not have any awareness of these nonverbal behaviors that are occurring.

A noun commonly used in many contexts and situations is *etiquette*, which is the acceptable or preferred conduct or procedure expected or observed in society or systems. Adapting to the virtual realm, we understand *netiquette* to represent the set of standards, expectations, or professional best practices for interaction, collaboration, and communication through electronic and virtual media (e.g., emails, video conferencing with Zoom, etc.) (Mintu-Wimsatt et al., 2010). For groups that may exist in a virtual realm or split time between virtual and face-to-face, a discussion about the expected netiquette for the group is recommended. This may be especially helpful in the digital age we all live in today because the roles, responsibilities, purposes, and perspectives we use the virtual platforms for may not automatically translate across all areas. Just as one would not expect that the etiquette for engaging in the face-to-face experience of being a member on a sports team will automatically translate to the same roles, responsibilities, and perspective if they are a member of a student in a classroom, the same is true in the virtual space. To help set members (and leaders) up for success, a conversation to clarify and address all expected netiquette is suggested as early as possible and likely will need review more than once to support transitional learning and adaptation of the expected behaviors and procedures.

Within the education system, universities are paving the way with concrete and published netiquette expectations in course syllabi. As with all groups and systems, the areas listed are offered as suggestions to consider, but are not meant to represent all groups. Leaders are invited to consider these areas as a starting point and create a list of expectations that adapts best to the population and setting where they will be facilitating the group. When possible, inviting additional suggestions from the members as a part of the first session may also be a powerful exercise to help reinforce and clarify expectations, establish norms, and begin inviting cohesion and relationships between and among members and the group as a whole.

- *Maintain the human connection.* Whether communicating verbally or nonverbally, always remember you are communicating with a fellow human.
- *Professionalism and ethical best practice remain.* Whether one is communicating in person or virtually, professionalism and ethical behavior are essential for the professional counselor-in-training.
- *Respect people's time and bandwidth.* When in the virtual group format, do your best to keep communication as concise as possible. The interactive and interpersonal engagement of all group members will likely flow differently in a virtual group versus an in-person group, and often there is a significant lack of nonverbal communication in virtual groups. Thus, virtual groups rely heavily on verbal communication more so than face-to-face groups will. Working to be inclusive of all members, concise verbal contributions are encouraged more so than what might be observed in a traditional face-to-face format. Note also that with virtual groups it is possible that there may be members joining from time zones that might be relevant for group members to be mindful of.
- *Be open to different styles and quality of writing and written communication.* When a group will infuse opportunities for asynchronous engagement, such as through posting discussions on a confidential or secured board and not rely solely on synchronous verbal communication, it is important to not be judgmental of the quality of the communication. Although writing is a common method of communication in the higher education environment, we do not all

communicate in the same way. Be open, understanding, and patient with regard to other's styles and quality of writing. Do your best to present your best work relevant to the topic on hand. Reduce and/or explain jargon or acronyms when used and strive for clear mechanics, grammar, and organization in all submissions. Work to be mindful of the setting the group is taking place in and not transfer acronyms or jargon that may not be synonymous. For example, abbreviated language that may be commonly used on Twitter influenced by the social media's character count limitation may not translate well to a group running in a virtual school setting that is focused on providing interventions or psychoeducational prevention.

- *Do not participate in bullying or incite arguments.* It is expected that different perspectives and viewpoints will be shared as a part of the learning process. Be authentic and genuine, just as you would be in person; however, be mindful of how written words, limited nonverbal communication, or truncated verbal communication might be misunderstood or misinterpreted. Maintain a respectful dialogue in the online forum, and invite offline conversations (in-person or telephone or private video conferences), as needed, to discuss topics in more detail.

- *Invite collaborative discussion with kindness and constructive feedback rather than dominant discussions.* We all have information, experiences, and examples to share and offer to enrich the group as a whole and its goals. Invite sharing of knowledge and expertise in an open and collective manner. Invite engagement and dialogue from all members rather than one-directional conversations with the leader and a member or a "fish bowl" between two members. Strive to consider different perspectives while receiving feedback and challenge yourself to respectfully offer constructive feedback to support the goals and growth of others in the group. Remember, the person(s) receiving the feedback retain the right to accept or not accept the feedback being offered. For some people, giving and receiving feedback may not be a new idea to them, but doing so as a member of a group with a different purpose and set of expectations may be a new experience. It may also be new to give and/or receive feedback in the online modality. The flow of conversations in an online group does not typically look or feel the same as it transpires in a traditional in-person setting. Invite and encourage members to ask questions, and to make note of immediate thoughts they may have when someone is speaking so they can refer to it later, and know that topics can be revisited at any time!

- *Confidentiality and privacy.* Mirroring expectations in a traditional in-person group, every member of the group is reminded to uphold confidentiality and respect the privacy of each member and the group overall. If concerns are raised, members should contact the facilitator immediately. While efforts to ensure confidentiality will be maintained, it is very difficult to do so regardless of whether one is working with students or adults. One maxim to consider is: "What is said in group, stays in group. What is learned in group, leaves group." In this perspective, members are encouraged to apply and share their own personal learning experiences as they engage with others in the world, but they are still asked and expected to uphold the privacy and confidentiality of what was said by themselves and by others.

- *Consideration of background and location.* Consider the location in your home or workspace where you set up for any virtual session. Regardless of whether it is for a meeting or for a group session, seek to identify an environment free of distractions during the allocated time. This may include being in a noise-free environment with limited distractions from family, coworkers, and possibly pets (notwithstanding an unexpected emergency). Consider the physical space. Does it provide ample room, lighting, overall comfort, resources, electricity/power access, acoustics, etc.? Does it meet your learning needs and support your active engagement? Does it provide a space to protect confidentiality to the best of your abilities? Being in public spaces such as outdoor coffee shops or parks, even if one is using headphones, may not provide or support the confidentiality required. Additional elements members and leaders may wish to consider in advance includes background images, eating/drinking during virtual sessions, and the overall appearance of them and the background environment, especially when engaging in the virtual environment from a personal space. Environments where we may be physically located when we need to join virtual groups or meetings do not always mirror or accurately illustrate the depths and capabilities of our unique selves. Members and leaders are reminded to be mindful and thoughtful when additional glimpses into personal spaces that we might not otherwise see are part of the reality in this digital age we are now all adjusting to.

GROUPS IN ACTION

Create 5 to 10 discussion questions that attendees can utilize to extend their learning. Questions should also facilitate discussion on how practitioners can put into practice what they have learned.

Example Questions

1. If you are counseling students using a virtual platform, what are some risk factors that you must be on the lookout for? And, if there is a student who presents with suicide ideation, what is the first thing that you should try and do?

2. How does your school or school district recruit students to participate in groups? Are parents' permission required to participate, or is there an opt-out process?

3. What are some user-friendly assessments and screening tools that could be used within a virtual environment to screen students for participation?

4. If some students do not want to use their cameras, should it be mandatory? Why or why not?

5. How can you go about using the chat/text feature when counseling students?

6. What grade or age level of students should be able to participate in virtual small groups? What brings you to this conclusion?

7. What is an appropriate number of students that should be in each of your groups? How long should these virtual sessions take place?

8. To what extent is resiliency a concept that is developmentally appropriate for all students PreK-12 and from all racial and cultural backgrounds?

9. Traditional groups in school settings help students with social, emotional, and behavioral issues. Which of these might be most easily addressed in a virtual environment?

10. What are some aspects of this session that are applicable to your work within your particular setting and what areas are you still in need of further exploration?

To better prepare school counselors for entry into the evolving PreK-12 landscape, counselor training programs are encouraged to consider identifying developmentally adaptable strategies to efficiently use and integrate technology. One suggestion is for counselor training programs to infuse a requirement in the clinical supervised internship experience for a minimum number of direct hours to be accrued engaging in this specific area of skill development. Several educators, counselors, administrators, students, and families have been forced to learn a new language abruptly so that they can navigate these dual-learning environments. One of the major challenges has been learning how to teach how to use the technology while differentiating the technology and still effectively teaching to achieve required student performance data benchmarks that directly connect to funding opportunities for many public districts nationwide. We must collectively acknowledge the additional stress that is likely compounding covertly for all roles within the PreK-12 schools regarding these abrupt changes in the educational environment. Many states offered minor modifications to evaluation and testing requirements at the end of the 2019–2020 academic year based on the global pandemic beginning to root itself in the United States in the March and April of 2020. However, during the 2020–2021 academic year many educators, counselors, and administrators experienced ambiguous or fluid requirements around testing and evaluation disseminated by state and federal government leadership. You may have a highly effective and skilled teacher, but if they are not as comfortable in a hybrid or virtual environment for any number of reasons, their evaluations and effectiveness data may illustrate different findings. Some of the essential skills to support best practices and efficient work in a school setting include:

- Understanding technology developmental readiness of each student in an educational environment
- Understanding different netiquette expectations that may reasonably be achieved at the different grade levels
- Recognizing different signs of technology-induced fatigue, anxiety, and types of stress among students as well as fellow adult colleagues within the school community
- Identifying if there are healthy coping strategies in place to assist with mitigating technology-induced fatigue.

It is also important to recognize and acknowledge the increased effects of stress for all individuals. For many children, adolescents, and adults, the stress-relieving habits and coping strategies they may have regularly employed prior to the pandemic may no longer be available. For example, often people would reference meeting up with friends by going out for a meal, having coffee, or engaging in another social activity as a way of supporting rebalancing and stress relief. In the wake of the global pandemic, these options may no longer be available to ensure the safety and health of each person, or they may be drastically modified as to what is attainable due to public health restrictions for businesses. For others, spending time with family may have been the strategy of choice, and due to restricted travel regulations or the vulnerable health of several population groups, visits may not currently be possible. As the United States and the world begin to settle into "the new normal" that requires increased distance, separation, restrictions, and isolation from friends, extended family, and others, many individuals are having extreme difficulties maintaining healthy levels of stress, balance, and overall wellness. Even after the health concerns of the COVID-19 pandemic reduce and become manageable, it is likely in this digital new age we live in that elements of the virtual transitions that have so dramatically and abruptly changed education, learning, communication, productivity, and the workforce will remain. Examples such as retaining virtual schooling and increasing education-related state and federal policies and requirements may be likely. Updates to training and licensing requirements in some states to demonstrate skill and knowledge acquisition for being effective in a virtual environment may be likely. And, continuing to use synchronous and asynchronous virtual delivery modes to offer continuing professional development, collaborate with broader stakeholder groups, and increase access to opportunities for more may likely continue.

Pulling It All Together

Drawing awareness and inviting a new perspective as to how and when various groups are commonly used in PreK-12 public schools can support best-practice efforts by counselors and more. As societal needs and issues become more challenging, it is incumbent upon the profession to consider implications for how to best proactively support the various roles within a school environment, including students, teachers, administrators, parents, counselors, and other staff and community stakeholders. Using an intentional dynamic group perspective will assist with inclusive and equitable actions empowering individuality, diversity, and efficient practices. School counselors' unique training to deliver prevention and intervention services as well as to work with children, adolescents, and adults primes them for being at the forefront of this effort to embrace a new framework that has implications for the entire school culture. Recognizing and engaging in the "power of group," even if the purpose is a task group, supports adaptive interpersonal communication and relationships, intrapersonal development and growth, efficient behaviors to achieve identified outcomes, and the mastery of essential life skills that can influence and inform citizenship in other areas of one's life. Positive influences are possible for individuals at all age levels as well as within the broader school culture and community.

DISCUSSION QUESTIONS

1. What ways have you used technology to support your daily or weekly efforts in your professional career? In your personal life? Are there examples of overlap?

2. How has technology helped you to engage with others in any type of group type? What may be some examples of how it has delayed or stalled processes?

3. How would you rate your digital literacy skills? Where are areas you could further develop? What are examples of specific resources you could use to help you develop these areas?

REFERENCES

Barbour, M. K., & Reeves, T. C. (2009). The reality of virtual schools: A review of the literature. *Computers and Education, 52,* 402–416.

Burbules, N. C., Fan, G., & Repp, P. (2020). Five trends of education and technology in a sustainable future. *Geography and Sustainability. 1*(2), 93–97. https://doi.org/10.1016/j.geosus.2020.05.001

Jain, G. (2020). Emerging trends of education during and post COVID 19: A new challenge. *Solid State Technology, 63*(Suppl. 1), 796–806.

Mintu-Wimsatt A., Kernek, C., & Lozada, H. R. (2010). Netiquette: Make it part of your syllabus. *Journal of Online Learning and Teaching, 6*(1), 264–267.

Miron, G., Shank, C., & Davidson, C. (2018). *Full-time virtual and blended schools: Enrollment, student characteristics, and performance.* National Education Policy Center. http://nepc.colorado.edu/publication/virtual-schools-annual-2018

8

Activities and Resources

A major theme throughout this book is a celebration of the intersection of flexibility, creativity, and intentionality that is possible through group work. To that end, we offer activities in this chapter and invite you to use these to actively engage your groups or to modify them to best meet your group goals. These activities can be adapted to multiple populations and types of groups, which is why we decided to dedicate a separate chapter to universally relevant activities and resources. Beyond activities, additional resources to inform and guide best practices and multicultural competencies are also included. Excerpts salient to the focus of this book are summarized below, along with the full reference.

Group Leader Preparation Self-Assessment for School Counselors or School Personnel

Directions: Consider the self-reflective questions and prompts provided below. Check all cells that best match your current self-assessment. Counselors are encouraged to consider this self-assessment tool to assist with monitoring awareness and identifying specific goals that will support their ethical best practice efforts when engaging in group work and group counseling or preparing/advocating for professional development needs.

	Task	Psychoed-ucational	Counseling	Therapy
Which culturally relevant groups have you had experience leading as a sole group leader?				
Which culturally relevant groups have you had experience leading as a coleader?				
Thinking about your school building, which types of groups have you observed intentionally using culturally relevant group practices to serve students?				

Thinking about your school building, which types of groups have you observed intentionally using culturally relevant group practices to serve the teachers/staff?				
Thinking about your school building, which types of groups have you observed intentionally using culturally relevant group practices to serve administrators?				
Which culturally relevant types of groups are most commonly used to address prevention needs/goals in your building?				
Which culturally relevant types of group are most commonly used to address intervention needs/goals in your building?				

What are some ways you advocate for culturally relevant group work within your school setting?

_____

_____

_____

TRATE My Group Framework Brainstorming/Planning Guide

What are examples of groups offered in your building that extend beyond intervention? What type of group is often used? What role(s) within the building are commonly a part of the group? What audience(s) do they serve? What is the duration and frequency of the group meetings? How do you know if the group was successful or effective in meeting its goals and objectives? Use the following TRATE My Group template to provide examples.

Example 1

Group Theme/Title: _____

T: _____

_____

_____

R: _____

_____

_____

A: _____

_____

_____

T: _____

_____

_____

E: _____

_____

_____

Example 2
Group Theme/Title: _____

T: _____

_____

_____

R: _____

_____

_____

A: _____

_____

_____

T: _____

_____

_____

E: _____

_____

_____

Group Work Progress Monitor

This self-assessment tool can be useful for monitoring progress and growth and to set professional development goals. This tool can be used by counselors-in-training as they are structuring their clinical experiences. It may also be helpful for practitioners grounded in a data-driven approach to enhance skills and knowledge for delivery services related to groups.

	I am knowledge-able	I am skilled	I am comfort-able	I need more training
To lead in general	4	3	2	1
To colead in general	4	3	2	1
To be a member of a group	4	3	2	1

To be a process observer	4	3	2	1
To plan and lead task groups	4	3	2	1
To plan and lead psychoeducational groups	4	3	2	1
To plan and lead counseling/ growth groups	4	3	2	1

Full-Length Training Videos and DVDs

Many videos are provided on electronic library databases with higher education institution library subscriptions. Reconnecting with the training program you completed or a local university with a counseling program may be helpful in accessing these resources. Counselor educators may find showing these videos or clips in training classes to be helpful. Individuals may also try contacting the vendors directly, because some sell these videos (e.g., ASGW has a catalog of DVDs and videos for sale through their organization).

Association for Specialists in Group Work DVD Catalog

- *Developmental aspects of group counseling: Process, leadership, and supervision*, Parts I–III (featuring Dr. Rex Stockton; manuals prepared by Dr. Kelly McDonnell), 2012.
- *Group counseling with children: A multicultural approach with children* (featuring Sheri Bauman and Sam Steen; manuals prepared by Nicole Buchheit and Linda Shealy), 2014.
- *Group counseling with adolescents: A multicultural approach* (featuring Sheri Bauman and Sam Steen; manuals prepared by Rachel Vannatta and Linda Feehs), 2012.
- *Group work: Leading in the here and now*, Parts I–III (featuring Dr. Peg Carroll; manuals prepared by Dr. Christine Suniti Bhat and Dr. Stephanie Eberts), 2012.
- *Leading counseling groups with adults: A demonstration of the art of engagement* (featuring Ed Jacobs and Christine Schimmel; manuals prepared by Ed Jacobs and Christine Schimmel), 2015.
- *Leading groups with adolescents* (featuring Janice Delucia-Waack, Allen Segrist, and Arthur M. Horn; manuals prepared by Dr. Amy Nitza), 2007.

Additional Titles Available in the Psychotherapy.net "Group Therapy" DVD Catalog

- *Adlerian parent consultation* by Jon Carlson
- *Children of the camps: The documentary* by Satsuki Ina
- *Understanding group psychotherapy with Dr. Irvin Yalom* (three-video series):
  - Volume I: Outpatients
  - Volume II: Inpatients
  - Volume III: An Interview
- *Group therapy: A live demonstration* by Molyn Leszcz and Irving Yalom

VARIOUS E-VENDOR PLATFORMS TYPICALLY AVAILABLE VIA UNIVERSITY SUBSCRIPTIONS

Adams, S., Conyne, R., & Wilson, F. (1999). *Task group demonstration learning through discussion.* Produced by the University of Cincinnati Media Services and Medical Center Public Relations and Communications. Producer, Malcolm Montgomery; director, Shawn Adams. Distributed by Microtraining Associates.

Cohen, J., & Whiteley, J. (1974). *Carl Rogers conducts an encounter group. Parts 1 & 2.* John Whiteley.

Cohen, J., & Whiteley, J. (1970). *Carl Rogers on facilitating a group.* John Whiteley.

Conyne, R., & Wilson, F. (1999). *Psychoeducational group demonstration a career development group for international students.* Produced by the University of Cincinnati. Producer, Dan Reeder; director, F. Robert Wilson; script, F. Robert Wilson et al. Distributed by Microtraining Associates.

Haley-Banez, L., Ivey, A., Ivey, M., & Oldershaw, B. (2002). *Group microskills encountering diversity.* Lynn Banez with Allen E. Ivey and Mary Bradford Ivey; producer, Bruce Oldershaw. Distributed by Microtraining Associates.

Hines, P., Stockton, R., & Winninger, J. (1991). *Developmental aspects of group counseling process, leadership, and supervision with Rex Stockton.* A coproduction of the Association for Specialists in Group Work, Indiana University Center for Human Growth, and Indiana University Television. Writers, Rex Stockton, Peggy Hines; senior producer/director, John Winninger. Distributed by Microtraining Associates.

Kottler, J. (1995). *Encouraging risk taking in groups presented by the Association for Specialist in Group Work.* Master presenter series. American Counseling Association.

Weinstein, R., & Carroll, M. (2010, September 24). *Group work leading in the here and now.* Produced by the Association for Specialists in Group Work in cooperation with the Fairfield University Media Center. Director/content expert, Rona Weinstein; producer, Marguerite R. Carroll. Distributed by Microtraining Associates.

YOUTUBE VIDEOS OR CLIPS FOR TRAINING AND PRACTICE

Jacobs, E., & Schimmel, C. (2013). *Group counseling common mistakes.* https://youtu.be/Le8tEIHD_hk

Schimmel, C. (2013). *Group counseling video #1 (application with REBT lens).* https://youtu.be/XYc_APlH7VY

Steen, S., & Bauman, S. (2014). *Group counseling with children: A multicultural approach with children* [clip]. https://youtu.be/bSOGSDGmNt4

Yalom, I. (2009). *Irvin Yalom inpatient group psychotherapy video.* https://youtu.be/05Elmr65RDg

APPENDICES

APPENDIX A. AMERICAN SCHOOL COUNSELORS ASSOCIATION

ASCA National Model Diamond, 4th edition, for use in training school counselors.

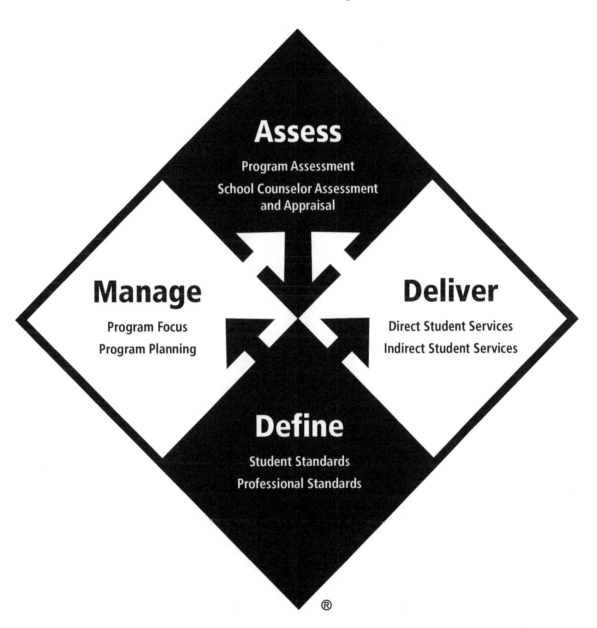

IMG A.1: American School Counselor Association, "ASCA National Model Diamond," schoolcounselor.org.

APPENDIX B. ASSOCIATION FOR SPECIALISTS IN GROUP WORK

The purpose of the ASGW Professional Standards for the Training of Group Workers (2000) and the ASGW Multicultural Competence and Social Justice Principles for Group Workers (2012) is to provide guidance to counselor training programs in the construction of their curricula for graduate programs in counseling (e.g., master's, specialist, and doctoral degrees and other forms of advanced graduate study). Specifically, core standards express the ASGW's view on the minimum training in group work all programs in counseling should provide for all graduates of their entry-level, master's degree programs in counseling, and specialization standards provide a framework for documenting the training philosophy, objectives, curriculum, and outcomes for each declared specialization program. In 2021, the ASGW consolidated best practices and guidelines to create the ASGW Guiding Principles for Group Work document. The framework and historical information presented offers "contemporary integration of ethical practice, contextual perspectives, and organizational values with the intent to guide group scholars and practitioners across varied disciplines and purposes" as they engage in group counseling intervention work in a global and 21st century landscape.

Definitions and Key Concepts

Collaboration: Group Workers assist members in developing individual goals and respect group members as co-equal partners in the group experience.

Consultation and Training With Other Organizations: Group Workers provide consultation and training to organizations in and out of their setting, when appropriate. Group Workers seek out consultation as needed with competent professional persons knowledgeable about group work.

Diversity: Group Workers practice with broad sensitivity to client differences including but not limited to ethnic, gender, religious, sexual, psychological maturity, economic class, family history,

Appendix B is adapted from:

R. Valorie Thomas and Debra A. Pender, "Association for Specialists in Group Work: Best Practice Guidelines 2007 Revisions," *The Journal for Specialists in Group Work*, vol. 33, no. 2, pp. 114–117. Copyright © 2008 by Association for Specialists in Group Work (ASGW). Reprinted with permission.

Anneliese A. Singh, et al., Association for Specialists in Group Work: Multicultural and Social Justice Competence Principles for Group Workers, pp. 2–3. Copyright © 2012 by Association for Specialists in Group Work (ASGW). Reprinted with permission.

C. J. McCarthy, et al., Association for Specialists in Group Work: Guiding Principles for Group Work, p. 2. Copyright © 2021 by Association for Specialists in Group Work (ASGW). Reprinted with permission.

F. R. Wilson, et al., Association for Specialists in Group Work: Professional Standards for the Training of Group Workers. Copyright © 2000 by Association for Specialists in Group Work (ASGW). Reprinted with permission.

physical characteristics or limitations, and geographic location. Group Workers continuously seek information regarding the cultural issues of the diverse population with whom they are working both by interaction with participants and from using outside resources.

Ethical Surveillance: Group Workers employ an appropriate ethical decision making model in responding to ethical challenges and issues and in determining courses of action and behavior for self and group members. In addition, Group Workers employ applicable standards as promulgated by ACA, ASGW, or other appropriate professional organizations.

Evaluation: Group Workers include evaluation (both formal and informal) between sessions and at the conclusion of the group.

Group Competencies: Group Workers have a basic knowledge of groups and the principles of group dynamics, and are able to perform the core group competencies, as described in the ASGW Professional Standards for the Training of Group Workers (Wilson et al., 2000). They gain knowledge, personal, personal awareness, sensitivity, and skills pertinent to working with a diverse client population. Additionally, Group Workers have adequate understanding and skill in any group specialty area chosen for practice (psychotherapy, counseling, task, psychoeducation, as described in the ASGW Training Standards).

Group and Member Preparation

- Group Workers screen prospective group members if appropriate to the type of group being offered. When selection of group members is appropriate, Group Workers identify group members whose needs and goals are compatible with the goals of the group.
- Group Workers facilitate informed consent. They communicate information in ways that are both developmentally and culturally appropriate. Group Workers provide in oral and written form to prospective members (when appropriate to group type): the professional disclosure statement; group purpose and goals; group participation expectations including voluntary and involuntary membership; role expectations of members and leader(s); policies related to entering and exiting the group; policies governing substance use; policies and procedures governing mandated groups (where relevant); documentation requirements; disclosure of information to others; implications of out-of-group contact or involvement among members; procedures for consultation between group leader(s) and group member(s); fees and time parameters; and potential impacts of group participation.
- Group Workers obtain the appropriate consent/assent forms for work with minors and other dependent group members.
- Group Workers define confidentiality and its limits (for example, legal and ethical exceptions and expectations; waivers implicit with treatment plans, documentation and insurance usage). Group Workers have the responsibility to inform all group participants of the need for confidentiality, potential consequences of breaching

confidentiality and that legal privilege does not apply to group discussions (unless provided by state statute).

Group Work: is a broad professional practice involving the application of knowledge and skill in group facilitation to assist an interdependent collection of people to reach their mutual goals which may be intrapersonal, interpersonal, or work-related. The goals of the group may include the accomplishment of tasks related to work, education, personal development, personal and interpersonal problem solving, or remediation of mental and emotional disorders.

Meaning: Group Workers assist members in generating meaning from the group experience.

Multicultural: The belief systems and typical daily activities of people from various diverse groups, and denotes that attending to the needs and values of these diverse groups ensures a more vibrant, dynamic, and empowered society overall. Examples of multicultural identities include (but are not limited to): gender identity and expression, race/ethnicity, sexual orientation, religious/spiritual traditions, ability status, migration status, age, and social class.

Oppression: The systemic, limited access to resources for an individual, group, or community due to multi-systems prejudice and discrimination (e.g., racism, sexism, heterosexism, classism, ableism, adultism, ageism).

Processing Schedule: Group Workers process the workings of the group with themselves, group members, supervisors or other colleagues, as appropriate. This may include assessing progress on group and member goals, leader behaviors and techniques, group dynamics and interventions; developing understanding and acceptance of meaning. Processing may occur both within sessions and before and after each session, at time of termination, and later follow up, as appropriate.

Professional Development: Group Workers recognize that professional growth is a continuous, ongoing, developmental process throughout their career.

- Group Workers remain current and increase knowledge and skill competencies through activities such as continuing education, professional supervision, and participation in personal and professional development activities.
- Group Workers seek consultation and/or supervision regarding ethical concerns that interfere with effective functioning as a group leader. Supervisors have the responsibility to keep abreast of consultation, group theory, process, and adhere to related ethical guidelines.
- Group Workers seek appropriate professional assistance for their own personal problems or conflicts that are likely to impair their professional judgment or work performance.

- Group Workers seek consultation and supervision to ensure appropriate practice whenever working with a group for which all knowledge and skill competencies have not been achieved.
- Group Workers keep abreast of group research and development.

Reflective Practice: Group Workers attend to opportunities to synthesize theory and practice and to incorporate learning outcomes into ongoing groups. Group Workers attend to session dynamics of members and their interactions and also attend to the relationship between session dynamics and leader values, cognition and affect.

Self Knowledge: Group Workers are aware of and monitor their strengths and weaknesses and the effects these have on group members. They explore their own cultural identities and how these affect their values and beliefs about group work.

Social Justice: The awareness of how social locations of social privilege and oppression influence group work process and dynamics, but also identifying ways to take action related to these social locations and the various social justice issues group members and workers experience (Singh & Salazar, 2010a, b, c).

Social Privilege: The power and advantage a dominant group is granted, entitled to, or born into that provides those individuals in the dominant group with the ability to sanction and/or have immunity based on the identities of gender identity and expression, race/ethnicity, sexual orientation, religious/spiritual traditions, ability status, migration status, age, and social class amongst others (Black & Stone, 2005).

Specialization Training in Group Work: includes knowledge, skills, and experiences deemed necessary for counselors to engage in independent practice of group work. Four areas of advanced practice, referred to as specializations, are identified: Task Group Facilitation, Group Psychoeducation, Group Counseling, and Group Psychotherapy. This list is not presumed to be exhaustive and while there may be no sharp boundaries between the specializations, each has recognizable characteristics that have professional utility. The definitions for these group work specializations have been built upon the American Counseling Association's model definition of counseling (adopted by the ACA Governing Council in 1997), describing the methods typical of the working stage of the group being defined and the typical purposes to which those methods are put and the typical populations served by those methods. Specialized training presumes mastery of prerequisite core knowledge, skills, and experiences.

Specialization in Task and Work Group Facilitation:
- The application of principles of normal human development and functioning
- through group based educational, developmental, and systemic strategies
- applied in the context of here-and-now interaction
- that promote efficient and effective accomplishment of group tasks among people who are gathered to accomplish group task goals.

Specialization in Psychoeducation Group Leadership:

- The application of principles of normal human development and functioning
- through group based educational and developmental strategies · applied in the context of here-and-now interaction
- that promote personal and interpersonal growth and development and the prevention of future difficulties
- among people who may be at risk for the development of personal or interpersonal problems or who seek enhancement of personal qualities and abilities.

Specialization in Group Counseling:

- The application of principles of normal human development and functioning
- through group based cognitive, affective, behavioral, or systemic intervention strategies
- applied in the context of here-and-now interaction
- that address personal and interpersonal problems of living and promote personal and interpersonal growth and development
- among people who may be experiencing transitory maladjustment, who are at risk for the development of personal or interpersonal problems, or who seek enhancement of personal qualities and abilities.

Specialization in Group Psychotherapy:

- The application of principles of normal and abnormal human development and functioning
- through group based cognitive, affective, behavioral, or systemic intervention strategies
- applied in the context of negative emotional arousal
- that address personal and interpersonal problems of living, remediate perceptual and cognitive distortions or repetitive patterns of dysfunctional behavior, and promote personal and interpersonal growth and development
- among people who may be experiencing severe and/or chronic maladjustment.

Trends and Technological Changes: Group Workers are aware of and responsive to technological changes as they affect society, and the profession. These include but are not limited to changes in mental health delivery systems; legislative and insurance industry reforms; shifting population demographics and client needs; and technological advances in Internet and other communication devices and delivery systems. Group Workers adhere to ethical guidelines related to the use of developing technologies.

Taking action: A central focus of social justice competency, both multicultural and social justice competency are ongoing processes of self-reflection, learning, and action. Because issues of privilege, power and exploitation are so insidious in the various systems of oppression that exist (e.g., racism, sexism, heterosexism, classism), group workers must take the time to identify specific ways in which privilege and oppression statuses and oppressive systems work.

When group workers seeking multicultural and social justice advocacy competence identify issues of privilege and oppression and oppressive systems operating within themselves (i.e., internalized oppression) and their group settings, they should: embrace their role as a social change agent; develop the skills to move towards making specific changes based on their knowledge and roles; develop ability to take action and make changes to group work practice, research, training, and advocacy; and identify issues of privilege and oppression that influence group workers and group members.

Therapeutic Conditions and Dynamics: Group Workers understand and are able to implement appropriate models of group development, process observation and therapeutic conditions. Group Workers manage the flow of communication, addressing safety and pacing of disclosures to protect group members from physical, emotional, or psychological trauma.

Values in Group Work: values and value-based beliefs provide a framework for how to conceptualize, apply. And evaluate the professional preparation, ethical practice, and process of group work. Examples of values offered by ASGW that can be observed through the practice of specialists in group work may include:

- Fidelity to diversity, equity, and inclusion
- Development of cultural sensitization, responsiveness, and competence, and the willingness to be informed by other cultures, communities, and disciplines
- Openness to innovative techniques, modalities, and delivery platforms
- Commitment to a holistic framework for the training, practice, supervision, evaluation, and research of group work
- Conviction that group work has specific, distinct, and unique benefits
- Belief that group work holds great potential to facilitate human growth, development, and healing in the robust interpersonal environment rather than individually
- Definable core knowledge base, clinical skills, and advocacy skills essential for competent group work practice
- Idiosyncratic ethical considerations across training, practice, supervision, evaluation, and research domains
- Research-informed practice
- Excellence through ongoing professional development that includes continuing education, supervision, and ongoing examination and adoption of culturally competent practices

REFERENCES

Black, L. L., & Stone, D. (2005). Expanding the definition of privilege: The concept of social privilege. *Journal of Multicultural Counseling and Development, 33*(4), 243-255.

McCarthy, C. J., Bauman, S., Coker, A., Justice, C., Kraus, K. L., Luke, M., Rubel, D., & Shaw, L. (2021, in-press). *Association for Specialists in Group Work: Guiding principles for group work.* https://asgw.org/resources-2/

Singh, A. A., & Salazar, C. F. (2010a). Six considerations for social justice group work. The Journal for Specialists in Group Work, 35(3), 308–319.https://doi.org/10.1080/01933922.2010.492908

Singh, A. A., & Salazar, C. F. (2010b). The roots of social justice in group work. The Journal for Specialists in Group Work, 35(2), 97–104. https://doi.org/10.1080/01933921003706048

Singh, A. A., & Salazar, C. F. (2010c). Process and action in social justice group work: Introduction to the Special Issue. The Journal for Specialists in Group Work, 35(2), 93–96. https://doi.org/10.1080/01933921003706030

Singh, A. A., Merchant, N., Skudrzyk, B., & Ingene, D. (2012). *Association for Specialists in Group Work: Multicultural and social justice competence principles for group workers.* https://asgw.wpengine.com.php73-37.phx1-1.websitetestlink.com/wp-content/uploads/2020/06/ASGW_MC_SJ_Priniciples_final_ASGW_Website_04_17_12.pdf

Thomas, R. V., & Pender, D. A. (2008). Association for Specialists in Group Work: Best Practices Guidelines 2007 Revisions. *Journal for Specialists in Group Work,* 33(2), 111–117. https://asgw.org/wp-content/uploads/2020/06/usgw297284-111..117.pdf

Wilson, F. R., Rapin, L. S., Haley-Banez, L., Conyne, R. K., & Ward, D. E. (2000). *Association for Specialists in Group Work: Professional Standards for the Training of Group Workers.* https://asgw.org/wp-content/uploads/2020/06/ASGW-Professional-Standards-for-the-Training-of-Group-Workers.pdf

APPENDIX C. COUNCIL FOR ACCREDITATION OF COUNSELING AND RELATED EDUCATION PROGRAMS (CACREP)

Upon completion of the group counseling course, students will have met the following professional standards through understanding knowledge/skills including:
2.F.6.a. theoretical foundations of group counseling and group work
2.F.6.b. dynamics associated with group process and development
2.F.6.c. therapeutic factors and how they contribute to group effectiveness
2.F.6.d. characteristics and functions of effective group leaders
2.F.6.e. approaches to group formation, including recruiting, screening, and selecting members
2.F.6.f. types of groups and other considerations that affect conducting groups in varied settings
2.F.6.g. ethical and culturally relevant strategies for designing and facilitating groups
2.F.6.h. direct experiences in which students participate as group members in a small group activity, approved by the program, for a minimum of 10 clock hours over the course of one academic term

Based on the 2016 CACREP Standards.

INDEX

ABOUT THE AUTHORS

Dr. Theresa Coogan, an associate professor, licensed professional school counselor and clinical mental health counselor, specializes in group work and professional training and identity development. Additional experience as an education consultant serving secondary, higher education, and state education authorities for more than a decade informs her understanding of the collective education pipeline and the systems within it. She actively seeks opportunities for service to local communities and the professional field through intentional community engagement and membership and leadership roles in professional organizations at the state, regional, and national levels. Dr. Coogan has published and presented research and conceptual work that centers on school counselor training, group work, gatekeeping for counselor training, and professional best practices.

Dr. Sam Steen, an associate professor and licensed professional school counselor, specializes in group work and cultivating Black students' academic identity development. He was a school counselor for 10 years and his practitioner experiences shape his research agenda, approach to teaching, and service. Dr. Steen is a fellow for the Association for Specialists in Group Work (ASGW), a division of the American Counseling Association. Recently, he received the Al Dye Research Award and the Professional Advancement Award both from ASGW in recognition of his outstanding efforts advancing the field of group work though research and development of new and innovative strategies for schools, families, and marginalized communities.